THE BEST VERSION OF YOU

HOW TO COACH YOURSELF AND OTHERS TO THE NEXT LEVEL OF SUCCESS

THE BEST VERSION OF YOU

HOW TO COACH YOURSELF AND OTHERS TO THE NEXT LEVEL OF SUCCESS

JOSH COATS

Published by Best Seller Publishing®, St. Augustine, FL
Best Seller Publishing® is a registered trademark
Printed in the United States of America.
ISBN:978-1-956649-47-5

This publication is designed to provide accurate and authoritative information with regard to the subject matter covered. It is sold with the understanding that the publisher is not engaged in rendering legal, accounting, or other professional advice. If legal advice or other expert assistance is required, the services of a competent professional should be sought. The opinions expressed by the authors in this book are not endorsed by Best Seller Publishing® and are the sole responsibility of the author rendering the opinion.

For more information, please write:
Best Seller Publishing®
53 Marine Street
St. Augustine, FL 32084
or call 1 (626) 765 9750
Visit us online at: www.BestSellerPublishing.org

TABLE OF CONTENTS

INTRODUCTION

I had just released my first full-length book. It hit number one on Amazon in six different categories. You'd think I would have been ecstatic! I should have been the happiest person in the world, having achieved this landmark goal in my life. But I wasn't. I was stressed. I was about as anxious as I had ever been in my entire life, and I was questioning everything.

I had built a multi-million-dollar business as a life and business coach who mostly worked with online entrepreneurs. I helped solopreneurs put together the right mindset and strategies to build their sales-based businesses online. I was about five and a half years into this career and was seen as one of the more influential leaders in my field. I wrote a book called *F*** Leadership* that was inspired by all of the times I had heard people say things like "Josh, I don't know if I can become successful because I'm not a good leader." Nine times out of ten, they were using the idea of "leadership" to replace something else they were insecure about and didn't know how to be honest about it.

So, I wrote a book addressing all of the things it actually takes to be a leader, to set the record straight. I poured everything into this book and was proud of every single word that went into it. People were raving about the content and leaving positive reviews left and right. So … why was I so unhappy?

Because I made the mistake that I warn everyone else against. You see, I was just a punk kid who detailed cars for a living and played in rock bands on the weekends. I was born in Tulsa, Oklahoma, and grew up outside of Wichita, Kansas. I thought I had life figured out. I would detail cars to pay the bills for my family while I grew my passion for music on the side. One day, my band would be big enough to travel the world and play music that inspired others and challenged them to chase their dreams.

Coming from a long line of preachers, I guess you could say it was in my blood to do something that I believed mattered. My family tree goes back to evangelists who came over on the *Mayflower*. I've always been obsessed with people and movements that have made the biggest impact on history. Being a white kid from Kansas didn't stop me from being drawn like a magnet to stories about people like Martin Luther King, Jr., Rosa Parks, and Harriet Tubman.

Inspired by bands like Coldplay, U2, and Switchfoot, I had envisioned myself being onstage and playing music that mattered. Music that made a difference in the world. Music that challenged the norms of society and questioned inequality and hatred. Music that aligned people with their purpose and passion.

But then my third son, Paxton, was born. On his very first night in the hospital, we found out that he had a heart defect and would need open-heart surgery. At six weeks old, he had his first procedure. Six months later, he had another. And then, when he was two and a half years old, we were told he might need a heart transplant. The first two procedures had been hard enough. When your body goes through something so traumatizing, it has no idea what to do and begins to empty fluids into your whole body. After each surgery, his body would double in size from the amount of fluids that were spilled out. It took a tube in his chest to drain out the fluids for over a week to get him back to his normal size. He would be hooked up to twenty machines after each procedure just to keep him alive.

And now we were looking at the possibility that he might need something even more severe, more risky, and less promising: a heart transplant. For the first time in my life, music no longer made sense. How could I continue traveling on the weekends, chasing after a passion that constantly took me further and further away from the family I loved? Meanwhile, there was no telling how long they would have to make sacrifices before it ever paid anything back. I told my band I was done. It was time to move on.

We were very fortunate that my son ended up not needing a transplant. A few months later he would undergo a twelve-hour surgery where his surgeon basically took his entire heart apart and put it back together. He is now ten and hasn't had to have any major procedures since!

But I still felt that it was time to move away from music. I had to find something that would both fulfill my creative passions and create a better life for my family—something that would make a difference in the world without taking me away from my babies. I had no idea what I was going to do, but I was determined to find something!

I remembered a random article I had read in a music magazine a few years before. It was an interview with Mark Tremonti, the guitar player from the early 2000s band Creed. He was talking about how he had no idea what he was going to do when Creed broke up. He didn't know what was coming next; he just knew that whatever was next, he wanted to be prepared for it. So Tremonti—someone who had made millions of dollars and could probably easily retire or find another band—decided to dig in and become the best version of himself. He started practicing six to eight hours a day and even hired a coach to hold him accountable to leveling up his skills.

I thought about that article and translated it into my current situation. If I didn't know what to do, I needed to commit to learning anything I could and trust that it would set me up for whatever my next move was. It was the first time I really got a hold of the principle I'm writing this book about. I realized this simple principle: the BEST version of me will figure it out.

As a business coach, I've watched person after person obsess over what they need to do to fix their business and then forget about the most important part of the business: themselves. Listening to podcast after podcast, I started to learn things about health, fitness, personal growth, and spirituality.

I started to find a new passion for just learning! Because I listened to six to eight hours of music each day while I detailed cars, I decided to give up listening to music at work and listen to podcasts instead. I felt such an adrenaline rush as I collected new information. I was more excited than I had ever been in my entire life!

In fact, I was having so much fun learning that I decided to write a mini book called *The Best You: Spirit, Soul, and Body*. This book never left the Notes app on my phone, but I had a blast writing it! Then I started a podcast called *The Best You*, just to start sharing what I was learning. I wasn't trying to make money. I wasn't trying to build a following or go viral. I was just so passionate about what I was learning that I felt the need to share it with others!

And then one day I came across a podcast in which John Maxwell was being interviewed. J Max (as I call him) was a name I had heard my entire life, growing up in a very religious household. My dad had several of his books, but I wasn't interested in reading, so I never knew what those books were about. As I listened to this podcast, I thought to myself, *This guy stole my dream!* He had found a way to take spiritual *and* growth principles and apply them to principles for living. One of the things that bothered me most about the religious circle I grew up in was watching so many people take the Bible and their beliefs in God and use them to manipulate others instead of empowering people.

There was so much emphasis on morals and such little emphasis on life lessons that, even though people in my church wanted to make a difference, no one knew how. I watched an entire generation of people in their sixties still complaining that they had a dream to reach the world but didn't feel like it was "God's timing" yet. As a twenty-five-year-old, I had realized that this was bullshit! In spite of my own fears and insecurities, I stepped out and started a band, to travel the world and chase my dreams. I didn't want to grow old still dreaming about what life could have been.

A few weeks after finding the Maxwell podcast interview, I saw an ad for a certification program. I could get certified as a life coach, speaker, and leadership trainer. I wasn't even sure what any of that meant, but something in me said, "I'm going to do that one day." Fast-forward a few months and one of my spiritual mentors, Cookie, asked me, "Josh, what do you want to do with your life?" I told her that I wanted to somehow combine spirituality and motivation, "kind of like John Maxwell," I said.

Cookie said, "You know, I have a personal friend who is on the President's Advisory Council of his certification program."

Say what?? I could hardly believe it. How could this be real? In my entire life, I've legit never had one single connection to things that gave me an advantage. Cookie offered to put me in touch with him, and I found myself on the phone with her friend Randy about a week later.

Our meeting was everything I'd hoped it would be. Talking to him, I could tell that he thought like J Max. He came from a church background, just like me, but seemed to think in a completely different way from anyone I had ever met. He seemed to really care about growth, creativity, and actually helping people. He gave me a personal recommendation for the certification program and, a few months later, I used my tax return to sign up.

From there, I had the hardest time in the world overcoming my own doubts, fears, and insecurities. But I kept using this simple principle: the best version of me will figure it out! Even though I only made $500 in my first year as a life coach, I went on to make $48K part-time in my second year and then $400K my third year, and since then, I have created a multi-million-dollar business.

But all of this started with making a very simple decision: to become the best version of me. And day after day, I've continued to live by that principle. Fast-forward to October 2019. I was in the middle of releasing my first full-length book. I understood that this could be a career-changing move to become a number one best-selling author. I had spent a year and a half writing, reviewing, editing, and finally getting this book released. It went live on Amazon at about 5 pm central time on a Friday night. When you submit your book to Amazon, it can be processed and go live in as little as forty-eight hours! In this case, it only took one hour before my book was processed and listed.

I immediately cancelled my plans for the evening. I got my laptop out and emailed my entire list to let them know it was live. I went on Facebook and Instagram to let my followers there know. I texted my friends, who also had large followings, and asked them to share with their friends. Within the first few hours, it had hit number one in a few categories. Holy shit, I wasn't expecting that. I thought it would take a few days to build up that kind of momentum.

I had hired a self-publishing company to help me promote the book, and they had checked out for the weekend. I panicked! Hitting number one was awesome and I should have been celebrating, but instead, I just felt all of the pressure in the world to find a way to keep the momentum going. Hitting number one was cool and all, but the goal of the book was to *stay* number one long enough that Amazon would take notice and start promoting the book on its Hot New Releases recommendations for others. I spent all evening emailing and posting.

I woke up the next morning and the book had hit number one in even more categories. It had even surpassed a few books that had been my favorite books to read. I watched my book pass *Good to Great* and *Building a StoryBrand*. Again, I should have been celebrating, but instead I kept feeling more and more pressure to keep the momentum going. I spent all weekend long hitting refresh on the charts, seeing how it was comparing to others, and trying to continue promoting it anywhere I could.

I woke up each day, checking the charts, obsessing over the numbers and categories, and ignoring my own mental health. I wasn't exercising, I wasn't doing my normal personal development, and my brain was running at 1000 mph all day and night. I found myself at the fair with my kids, hitting refresh on the reports and checking emails while I waited in line instead of being present with them.

Several weeks later, the hype had passed. I had an international best seller, but I felt lost. I had spent around $20K self-publishing and promoting a book that we were selling for $1 to help it get momentum on Amazon (it was just a digital release at first). I had spent the last several months promoting the book instead of doing my virtual training groups and coaching. I was trading out $200 sales (my average online course fee) for $1 sales. Sales for my groups were down because that's what happens when you're not promoting them. I had a fat check I needed to write the IRS for some taxes from the year before, and I was just a few months away from moving

THE BEST VERSION OF YOU

into the dream house that me and my girlfriend were building, which would bring on more expenses and more pressure to keep performing.

I don't know what happened, but somehow the fear of these financial pressures just took over. I felt like I was going to lose my mind. I couldn't stop thinking about the tax bill, how I was going to bounce back from a few down months in sales, and how I would be able to afford our new house with my business struggling like this! On a scale of one to the world is going to come to an end and I might lose everything and be homeless, I was feeling like a nine. My body was drained of all energy. I was over-obsessing about what to post on social media and what kind of promotions to run. It was like everything I had learned in growing a multi-million-dollar business was forgotten.

And then I made a new connection with a fitness trainer and mindset coach, Chris Downing. He had created workout programs for an online health and fitness company that I've done tons of business trainings for. I invited Chris to be a guest on my podcast, and he was happy to come on.

This episode saved my life. Chris talked about what he calls Old Self versus New Self and how our lives are a constant challenge of growing past our old habits and beliefs. It was the perfect person at the perfect time. While interviewing him, I realized that, in my book launch, I was so caught up in the numbers and charts that I had actually lost sight of the very thing my entire business had been built on: personal growth.

I woke up the next morning and went to the couch with my journal. I started the day off with meditation and affirmations. I still had the worries over the tax bill and my decreased sales in my head. I still didn't have a solution, but I told myself, *The best version of you will figure it out.* While I had understood this principle for years now, this was the first time I put these specific words together.

I realized that this was going to be a tough battle, but I also realized that the *worst* version of me didn't stand a chance at all! If I was going to get myself out of this mess, it was going to take the *best* version of me. Over and over again throughout the day, when I would think about that tax bill or my sales, I would just stop and repeat to myself, *The best version of you will figure it out.* I still didn't have a solution, but I was starting to regain my

7

confidence. I was starting to feel like my old self again. I still had a crazy tax bill and a sales slump to fix, but I was slowly worrying about it less and less. I was beginning to enjoy the fact that I was alive and had so many amazing things in my life!

Day after day I woke up, did my morning routine, and repeated over and over to myself: *The best version of you will figure it out.* And about two weeks later, my sales started to increase. I made a few high-ticket sales that wiped out the tax debt. I started to feel like myself again. My energy levels were coming back. And I was more passionate about my work than I had ever been. Within a month of working on the *best* version of me, the *worst* version of me was a thing of the past.

Now, let me just say that all problems are not fixed in one month. Let me remind you that, prior to this, I had spent six years working on the best version of myself and growing a business. Not everyone has built a business successful enough to make that big of a tax payment with a few sales. You might be trying to grow a business from scratch, you might be trying to lose a significant amount of weight, or you might be trying to heal from a bad relationship. I can't make any promises on how long it will take to fix your problems, but I can promise you this: whatever problems you're facing today, no matter how big or small, the *worst* version of you stands no chance. If any version of you can fix this mess and crawl out of this space, it's the *best* version of you!

I've always said that we are all about three to six months away from either the best version of ourselves or the worst version of ourselves. If you're broken, you can find incredible healing with about six months of sowing into your best self. And no matter how successful, happy, or powerful you are, you can turn back into the worst version of yourself in as little as six months of ignoring what got you to where you are!

When I found my best self again, I realized that the tax payment, the sales slump, and the pressure of my house were really only about a four out of ten problem. But the worst version of me had turned it into a forty out of ten problem. You would be amazed at just how small your problems really are compared to the power you have living on the inside. The problem is that most people have spent so much time ignoring and hiding from their best self that they have become something that is so far from their true self.

Your worst version is constantly overexaggerating everything you're facing in life because that version of yourself is just so weak and powerless. Your worst version sees scarcity where your best version sees abundance. Your worst version sees problems where your best version sees solutions. Your worst version sees fear where your best version sees a challenge. Your worst version sees all of your weaknesses where your best version sees all of your strengths.

Regardless of what you are facing today, I believe that this book will teach you just how powerful you are! Whether you're trying to get out of debt, find your career path, start your own business like I did, or just find happiness, these principles will help you to achieve whatever you want in life. That's because, as the most basic life coaching principle states, everything you need in life is already living on the inside. And as one of my teachers, Christian Simpson, always said, "The only difference between the successful and the unsuccessful is not their potential but rather their awareness of their potential."

For over seven years now, I have been a student of the principles of life and business that help individuals become the best version of themselves. I always use these principles to coach myself first, but I would be selfish not to pass those principles on to others.

The point of this book is to teach you how to coach yourself through your doubts and fears and insecurities. But I'm asking you, and even challenging you, to keep in mind how you can use these principles to coach others. Whether you are building a business, leading a team, or volunteering in your community, these principles are needed. Every one of these principles is what I would call a universal principle, meaning it will apply to every area of your life.

But I also ask you, as I ask the coaches in my certification program, to not try to teach this content if you're not willing to live it first. Don't add this book to your list of recommendations if you aren't also digging in and making it your own philosophy.

If I have one complaint about my own industry, it's that there are too many people sharing principles they haven't lived, and too many people claim to be experts about things they've never really worked out themselves.

In this book I'm going to teach you everything I've learned and used to coach myself and others to find the next level of success. Whatever area of life you are seeking a new level of success in, please know that it will always be an inside journey first. And if you want to help others, you have to teach them to do the inward work as well.

Imagine if you could become more aware of your potential than you are of your limits. Imagine waking up each day with confidence and feeling fully equipped to take on every single challenge that life has to offer. This isn't some type of positivity message that teaches you how to avoid your problems and pretend everything is going to work out. I'm talking about tapping into your inner potential, the version of you who knows how to solve those problems, not avoid them.

My goal is to teach you to become consciously aware of every good thing that is already living inside you and to use that to overcome your doubts, face your fears, and live beyond your insecurities.

This book will help you discover your dream, chase your dream, and eventually live out your dream. And then, as a result, you will have the tools you need to help and coach others to find and live out their dreams.

My name is Josh, and I'm Your PUSH Coach.

LET'S DIG IN!

PS: You can grab a free signed copy of the paperback and the PDF workbook for this book by going to www.joshcoats.com

1

LAW OF OWNERSHIP

When I first joined my leadership and coaching certification, the first assignment that was given to me was to read a book by John Maxwell (*The 21 Irrefutable Laws of Leadership*) three times before I was allowed to do anything else.

I was pissed. I had just given a $1,000 deposit to get enrolled, and the first thing they wanted me to do was spend more money on a book and read something that was available to the public? Plus, I was someone who had avoided reading my entire life. The only reason I got into this program was because of my passion for listening to podcasts, but reading was something I had hated my entire life. My brother and I used to jam out to a song by the band Switchfoot called Chem 6A, where the verse says multiple times, "I don't wanna read the book, I'll watch the movie."

Pissed as I was, I ordered a used copy of the book from Amazon for seven or eight dollars. When the book came in, I sat down at my desk to get started. The first chapter blew my mind and changed my life forever.

The first chapter was called "The Law of the Lid" and basically explained that we all have a lid on our level of leadership and that our success in life is dependent on our ability to learn, improve, and raise this lid to another level. In other words, if your leadership level is currently a four out of ten, the only way to have more success in life is for you to learn and develop more skills to become a five, six, and so on.

In this moment I had what some would call an aha moment, but I feel like I had an actual encounter with my Creator. I went into a trance-like state and saw my entire life flash before me. I grew up in small churches that were very close-minded and had listened to pastors and leaders my whole life complain that the church would grow more if more people would volunteer, if more people would show up on time, and if more people would tithe.

I had also played music for most of my life and would hang out at local guitar shops on my days off. I heard owners say over and over that they couldn't compete with Guitar Center because Guitar Center stayed open too late, let people play their guitars and drums too loud, and was open on weekends.

I have friends who used to own a coffee shop, and one of them would always complain that they couldn't compete with Starbucks because everyone just wanted sugar coffee and to go through a drive-through and get quick coffee that was low-quality.

In this moment, I realized that everyone I had been surrounded by for my entire life had always blamed others for their lack of growth and success.

I never heard a pastor say, "Well, the church hasn't grown in years, so I guess I need to learn more about leadership, become a more effective communicator, and do more community outreach to make our name known."

I never heard a guitar store manager say, "I guess we could hire someone to work weekends so we could be open on the days that people are free to shop. And I guess maybe it would be a good idea to let people turn up the amps and actually see what the instruments sound like before they buy them."

The coffee shop could have easily created a few options for people who preferred sweeter drinks and could have easily served their cold brew through a drive-through!

I had spent my twenties detailing cars for a living and working my ass off in hot summers and cold winters. I didn't have any paid time off and had to work sick on several occasions. When my youngest son went through his open-heart surgeries, I had several weeks where I stayed up with him in the hospital all night and then went to work and detailed cars on almost no sleep. I did all of this to make just enough money to barely scrape by. We had bills stacked up that were all late, and I couldn't even afford to buy my kids new clothes for school.

And in this moment, I realized the most important thing I could possibly pass on to you: that this entire mess that felt so completely awful and unfair was all my fault.

I had created this mess, not anyone else. I'm the one who chose not to go to college. I'm the one who kept detailing cars instead of taking a job in graphic design that paid less but may have created more long-term opportunities. I'm the one who started up my own business on several occasions but quit after a month or two when the excitement wore off.

I had created this mess.

But here's the good news: if I was the one responsible for creating the mess, it also meant that I was the only one who could *fix* the mess. I didn't need to wait for the perfect time or the right opportunity or some type of lucky break. I ultimately had the power to create whatever I want with my life with the choices I make and the chances I'm willing to take.

I made a promise right then and there that I would *never* blame anyone for my lack of success again. From then on, I would take full responsibility for everything in my life. If I didn't like something in my life, I would learn what I needed to learn and do what I needed to do to fix it. Even if I didn't know *how* it was my fault, I would still own it.

And that is why I took John Maxwell's principle of the Law of the Lid and personally coined it as the Law of Ownership. Because that word means so much more to me. I have to take ownership for where I am but also where I eventually want to be.

If you're reading this, you are taking the first step in taking control of your life. You might be in a terrible financial situation, you might have a business or career that is failing, or you might have a relationship that is broken. You might be experiencing incredible success but still feeling "stuck." I have found that high performers tend to do enough work to get to the top of the mountain but then sometimes feel lost, wondering, *What's next?* Wherever you are, reading this book is the start of taking action toward becoming the person who creates success after success. You are about to learn how you can take your next step and *keep* stepping.

If you make the decision right now to *act* on what you read, your life can change forever. By taking responsibility for my life, I was able to build a multi-million-dollar business, even though I only made two sales and $500 in my entire first year. Every time I had a consultation that didn't turn into a client, I went home and took ownership. I used it as motivation to read and study more.

I'll never forget the first event that I put on. I had some experience in events from playing in a band but also from several years of volunteering at church. I had helped my brother put on several youth events and had also served as the creative director at a church. The training I went through taught us that we should invite all of our friends to join us for a local mastermind. At the end of six weeks, we were supposed to ask our friends to help us put on an event. If we had six to ten people in our mastermind study and each one brought three or four people, we'd end up having twenty to thirty people. I was able to get four people to join my free mastermind, but with only four people, if one or two people couldn't make it, well, it was just me and one other person. That was a little awkward. But I was trusting the system. So now I needed to put on an event. I needed a venue, and the shop my friend was letting us use for our mastermind wasn't going to work. It was a little run-down, and I wanted this event to look professional.

I went to visit my friend Evan, who was a new Realtor. Like me, he was just getting started and trying to figure out how to get his business up and off the ground. I was telling him about my event, and he mentioned that the realty office he worked at had a meeting room upstairs that they used for small get-togethers. The building was in a really nice part of town, and from the outside, it looked like it was probably a really nice building. He offered to give me an introduction to his boss, who oversaw the Keller Williams Realtors in the area. Turns out, she was really big into personal growth and loved the idea of me doing a meeting there. She offered to let me use the room for free if I let Evan attend for free. Deal!

I started to piece together some other details. I knew that at the end of the event, I wanted to pitch my next mastermind, the first one I was going to charge for. One of my mentors had taught me that you really need to have a killer offer. I had one friend who had a start-up bakery and another friend who had a start-up coffee shop. I asked each of them if they would donate some of their products for me to give away, and then I would purchase more for people who bought my program. The idea was I could serve the coffee and cookies for free and then, at the end, I would offer a pound of coffee and a dozen cookies as a bonus for joining my group. Even looking back, I'm still impressed with the creativity I put into this. I was imagining people eating these delicious cookies and thinking, *Wow, where can I get more of these?* Then I would give my pitch and they would have a chance to both learn with me *and* get more cookies. It seemed brilliant.

I asked a friend from my church who had been a barista if she would come and serve coffee. I offered her a free ticket to the event for helping out. Then I got someone from the church to come and run the slides for me so I could be focused on the presentation. I had my dad come and oversee parking, so people knew exactly where to go. My sister helped out by giving out handouts and greeting people as they arrived.

Let's talk about promoting. My mentor challenged me to meet with business owners and get them to sponsor the event in exchange for free tickets for their employees. I got one company to sponsor, and they said they would send five of their employees. I called up a buddy who used to work with me and does photography. I asked if he would make a promo video for me if I detailed his car. His wife had a birthday coming up, so he was happy to do a trade-off if I would detail her car.

I told him, "I only need five minutes of your time. I'll knock out the video in one take." I showed up at a local outdoor shopping spot downtown so we could shoot at a nice little spot outside a coffee shop. He got things set up, hit record, and I nailed it. One take. He looked at me, surprised, and said, "People always tell me they can do it in one take and then it takes five to ten. People always overestimate what they can do on camera. But you nailed it. Do you maybe want to do one more, just in case?"

So, I did one more, just to humor him. But I had written out everything I wanted to say and gone over it in my head all day until I showed up. I was prepared. I was doing everything I could have possibly done.

Sounds like my first event was probably a hit, right? Well, eight people showed up. That was a bummer, but I still had a chance. If I could get four of them to sign up, I could make $1,000, and that would be a whole week of detailing cars.

I killed the presentation. I had been practicing day and night for weeks. At the end, I offered the chance to work with me in a mastermind study for six weeks. The cost would be $250, and anyone who signed up would also get a pound of coffee and a dozen of those delicious cookies. And then my boss from the detail shop stood up and said, "I'll throw in a free gold detail for anyone who buys Josh's training."

A gold detail was worth $200 to $280, depending on the size of your car. A $200 auto detail, a pound of local coffee, and a dozen of the best cookies you've ever tasted. Just like all of those times at the coffee shop, I was only paid in pats on the back that night. Not one single person signed up.

I'm crying as I type this, and I don't really know why. I guess because I'm remembering the pain I had to endure those first few years. Maybe I'm realizing, even as I type this, just how grateful I am for that thirty-year-old kid who was willing to do what I'm about to tell you.

I went home and cried. And I was pissed.

Why don't people care about personal growth? Why are people so cheap? Why doesn't anyone get this? I thought to myself all night long. I couldn't sleep. I finally passed out for a few hours and then woke up at six in the morning with these words in my head: the Law of Ownership.

I remembered the promise I had made to myself and God. I would never blame anyone else for my lack of success. The hardest part of the Law of Ownership is when you feel like you've done everything you know to do, and it still isn't enough. But I decided to trust. I decided to at least admit that I didn't know what I didn't know, and that meant I needed to learn more.

I bounced back with fire and decided to do a virtual version of the event for people out of town who couldn't make it. I had moved a few times in my life, so I had friends in Kansas and Missouri and maybe some of them would want to listen. So, I did the event again over a conference phone line (we didn't have Zoom at the time). This time, only four people showed up, but because it was over the phone, it didn't really cost me anything and didn't take any preparation. I was less mad and more determined.

I started wondering if maybe people in Tulsa still saw me as an auto detailer and were having trouble seeing me as an authority on personal growth. So, I went to social media. I started reaching out to people from my old hometowns who only knew what I was posting on social media. I lined up a few calls and actually signed a few clients. I then asked my new paying clients to help me put on another event. This time, I would have it in Kansas, where it seemed like I had a few people who were actually willing to pay me.

I put on another event, this time in another state. I promoted it on social media to all of my old friends and family. This time, I charged for the event. At the last event, I had pretended to charge and then gave everyone free tickets because no one would buy one. Plus, I knew I would need gas money. I ended up selling twenty tickets! Not a huge growth from eight, but this was twenty paying people, and only half of them were people I knew. The other half were people my new clients had invited.

I gave the same presentation, but this time with no coffee or cookies. This time, the mastermind study with me would all be over the phone. That day, I had a few people join my mastermind and another person pay me for one-on-one services. I walked away with $800. Just to remind you, I would have detailed twenty-eight cars over four days in 100-degree heat on a typical day to make $800. This $800 was like someone hugging me and saying, "You can do this!"

It was my first major win. More than a year after my start date, I needed it bad!

Do you want to hear something crazy? Looking back, it is *so* easy to see why my first event sucked so bad. I did *all* of the right things but just didn't have an audience of paying customers yet. I was trying to sell to people who were friends and family. Most of them didn't have $250. The ones who did didn't want to spend six weeks being mentored by their brother/ brother-in-law/co-worker. I couldn't see it then. And that is why the Law of

Ownership is so important. There are so many things that your future self will see as so obvious. If we aren't careful, we are so attached to the results we want today that we miss the chance to learn the lesson we really need to learn in order to get the results we want tomorrow.

I could have given up. I could have said, "I did everything they told me to do, and it didn't work." But I chose to trust that the process of learning and growing would give me the answers I needed *in time*. That's what this entire book is about. It's learning to take ownership and *trust* that the lessons will be revealed in time. You aren't going to get what you want today because you want it. Just wanting it isn't enough. You have to be willing to fight for it. Most of the time, that fight will happen inside your own head and heart.

You don't have to know it all. You don't have to figure it all out. But you do have to invest time, energy, and patience into becoming the *best* version of yourself. The best version of you will figure it out!

COACHING QUESTIONS

Fill in the blanks below.

_____ am the only one who is responsible for the mess in my life.

If I am the only one who created the mess, then I am the only one who can _____ the mess.

If you make the decision right now to _____ on what you read, your life can change forever.

If you really want to build a better life for you and your family, you have to embrace the fact that you are a _____.

You don't need anyone else's _____, and you really need to stop looking for their approval.

2

HEAD BELIEFS VERSUS HEART BELIEFS

When I made the decision to give up my eight hours of listening to music to listen to podcasts instead, I made a decision that changed my life forever. At the time, I didn't understand what was really happening. I thought I had just found something I enjoyed and that was why it was so exciting and empowering.

But now that I have had several years of training and have studied the topic of mindset and beliefs, I understand that something was happening on a larger scale altogether.

One of the first things I learned in life coaching was that our beliefs drive our behavior. Will Durant said in his book *The Story of Philosophy*, when discussing the ideas of Aristotle, "We are what we repeatedly do." And this is a great quote, but it's not a full truth. It's actually only a half-truth.

We are what we repeatedly do, but we repeatedly do what we really believe on the inside. People spend billions of dollars every year trying to change their health by trying to find a better system, a way to be more motivated, or a different diet. But the reality is, until someone believes they can lose weight, no attempt to change their behavior will be very successful.

In the same way, people are spending billions of dollars each year on business coaching, social media advice, websites, and lead generation, all trying to find the right system that will finally give them the breakthrough they want in their business. But because they don't understand this very simple principle, they find themselves paying for training they don't use or sabotaging the whole process and then blaming others.

Spending your time and energy trying to change your habits can work, but only if you have the willpower to force it. Some people do, but most don't. When you take the time to reprogram your beliefs, all of a sudden the actions aren't very difficult. Posting content to Instagram isn't as big a challenge when you believe with all of your heart that it's going to lead to the success you want, even if this individual post falls flat and gets no engagement.

Building a website or writing a book becomes a lot easier when you don't *need* it to give you the success you want, and you just truly believe that you are going in the right direction and living from your heart and purpose. Putting all of your energy into changing your habits is always most effective when it is combined with working on your beliefs.

As I'm writing, I am going through some rebranding in my business. I'm pivoting to help more life coaches with their branding. In doing so, I've been reflecting on my first year as a life coach. I will never forget just how powerful that first year was. Looking back, I can see just how bad I wanted to share my message with the world. I wasn't looking to make a million dollars or be a best-selling author. I just wanted to make a difference and change lives.

I got on every single call with this burning desire to help someone transform their life. The reality is, my first year in business was such a huge disaster. I failed over and over and over. But my desire to help others fueled me to keep reading, keep listening, and keep growing. I truly believed that I was on the right path, so I didn't need it to "work."

I can still remember speaking at live events for eight people and speaking on Zoom calls for four people. While I hated seeing such a small turnout, I was so fueled by my passion that I gave everything I had. I didn't need results because I was fueled by my purpose and passion. That made it easy to show up even when I didn't have the "right" plan or the "perfect" strategy.

I had played sports my whole life. I was never the best, but I was always one of the best because my dad had coached me at a young age and taught me to give everything I had. At the end of basically every practice in every sport I ever played was something called conditioning. This was usually around thirty minutes of running sprints (short runs at your fastest speed). One thing I can still remember is just how crazy it was that I could always beat people who were much faster than me.

What most people would do was run as fast as they could for the first five to ten minutes. But after that they would start to slack off as they felt more tired. I still don't know exactly where I learned this from, but I had a different mindset than they did. Maybe it was because I was the youngest in my family and always had to work twice as hard to keep up with my older brother, who was much bigger, stronger, and faster than me. Maybe it was because me and my brother would play basketball as kids with the teenagers from our church and had to work harder to keep up. For whatever reason, I knew how to dig in, even when I was winded and tired, and I found a way to run as fast as I possibly could, even after the initial five to ten minutes. In fact, by the time twenty-five to thirty minutes came around, I would be outrunning people by as much as 5 to 10 yards.

I remember one specific drill we did in football where we would run from the end zone to the 10-yard line. Then we would turn around and run back. Then we would turn and run to the 20-yard line. Then we would turn and run back. The sprint would grow by increments of 10 yards until we got to the last run, which went from one end zone to the other for a total of 100 yards. On the very last run, there was one guy who had been taking it easy for the last twenty minutes and was sick of watching me win, so he decided to sprint as hard and fast as he could. Now remember, I had been sprinting as hard and fast as I could the entire time, so he should have been better rested than me and should have smoked me on the last sprint if he just tried. But I heard him coming up on me, and I dug in. I found another gear and kicked it into an even faster speed. After about 20 yards of him trying to keep up with me, I heard him gasp and slow down because he couldn't handle keeping up with my speed for that long.

Why is it that I could outrun all of these players who were faster than me? It was all in my head. It couldn't possibly have been my talent or skill. Remember, these were people who were faster than me. But their mindset was, I'll run fast until it hurts. My mindset was, I'll run fast even if it hurts.

An analogy that might make more sense to you is the key analogy. Because I have a lot of women in my training groups, I have a good time making fun of myself and making men the butt of a lot of my jokes. As a man, if I can't find my keys, I look in the two places the keys are supposed to be. But when I don't find them, my response is, "Babe, I can't find the keys. I looked everywhere."

When my wife Jenny looks for the keys, she doesn't just look in the two places they are supposed to be. She's smart enough to know that they didn't walk away, so they have to be somewhere. So, she looks *until* she finds the keys.

When it comes to success in any area of your life, you have to approach it like a woman looking for the keys. You can't just look in a few places and say you tried everything. You have to look until you find it. In other words, success starts with a decision to go until you succeed.

Here's the problem: your subconscious mind is looking for a way to stay safe. Deep inside, you know exactly what kind of work it will take to become the person you need to become to get what you really want, so you're looking for an out.

The hardest part of success in your business or any other area of life will be fighting the inner battle of wanting to give up. What makes it even harder is the fact that the battle happening on the inside can make it feel like you are being untrue to yourself. It's one thing to go against friends and family (which can also be hard), but it's an entirely different thing to go against what feels like your own true self.

The first thing you need to know about this battle is that you are *not* fighting against your true self. You are only fighting against your old self. What I'm about to teach you is something that should be taught in every school in the world but, unfortunately, was only taught to me when I went through life coach training. I would say 99 percent of people go through life not even understanding their own physiological makeup, and *that* is what makes life hard.

I'm going to take some time to teach you what is happening inside your brain and your body, and the rest of this book is full-blown training on all of the ways I found to fight the battle to create my new self.

UNCONSCIOUS LIVING

In training more than forty thousand entrepreneurs who have social-media-based businesses, one of the things that I hear most is that posting on social media and doing online sales doesn't feel authentic. It makes them feel gross and icky.

The reality is, everything you do in life that goes against your old self feels icky because it feels like you are trying to "fake" your way into something new. And the constant saying of "Fake it till you make it" isn't helping anyone.

If you can convince yourself that you have to be fake to get what you want in life, you will almost always choose to quit instead. None of us want to be fake.

So, I help people to learn the difference between their head voice and their heart voice. Both are living on the inside, but only one of them is the *truest* version of you.

I believe that we are a three-part being. We are a spirit (or heart or soul), we have a mind, and we live in a body. All three are incredibly important, but not knowing their purposes can make life very difficult.

I believe in an infinite Creator. I grew up calling it "God" but also know that many people call this higher power "Universe" or "Spirit," among other names. I couldn't care less what you choose to call it, so for the sake of including everyone, I like the name Infinite Intelligence (adopted from my favorite book, *Think and Grow Rich* by Napoleon Hill).

I believe that our spirit—or heart, as I will refer to it moving forward—is the infinite part of us that has always been and will always be. I don't pretend to know where it was before this life or where it's going afterward. You can have that debate somewhere else. But I do believe that this part of us is in constant contact with our Creator. I believe we have a constant flow of light, energy, wisdom, and creativity that we can draw on at any time if we just know how to access it. We'll get into that in just a minute.

Our mind is one of the most misunderstood parts of this process. I believe it was given to us by our Creator as a tool to use. But when you don't know how to use a powerful machine, it can do a lot more harm than good. Our mind has a few different parts to it. I consider myself a lifelong learner, so I still have a lot of learning to do on this subject, but I want to break down what I do know that has helped me.

The three parts I want to talk about are the conscious mind, the subconscious mind, and our emotions.

Let's start with the subconscious, since it's the most misunderstood. The subconscious mind is like a computer: it has a hard drive where it can store infinite thoughts, experiences, and past feelings. Its main job is to protect and to perform. It is designed to protect you from possible threats and perform tasks on autopilot that no longer need your attention.

If you were a caveman, these two purposes would actually go hand in hand. If you saw a saber-toothed tiger for the first time, your subconscious would first send an alert that says, "We don't know what this is, so we need to assume it's dangerous." The second signal, coming less than a split second later, would say, "Then we better get the hell out of here," which would put you into a dead sprint for the nearest cave. This is where we get the term fight or flight.

Here's the biggest problem with our subconscious mind: it was designed for an age that most of us no longer live in. It was designed to keep you safe from actual threats, but it was not designed to process whether new things actually are a threat or not. In other words, every time you encounter something new, you get an immediate signal that will try to get you to run and hide. If you are living in an industrialized country where there are no sabertooth tigers or wild animals roaming the streets, this part of you isn't needed as much as it once was. One of the key elements on your road to success will be how much time you're willing to spend upgrading this computer. Like a phone or computer, you can't run new programs on old software or hardware. This book is going to serve as a manual on how to upgrade your software, but you still have to be willing to follow the instructions and see it through.

I like to use a smoke detector as an example of how our subconscious works. Have you ever had your smoke detector go off at your house, only to find out that it was a false alarm? I would be willing to bet that, for most people reading this, the alarm was false ten times more often than it was legit. None of you is stupid enough to grab all of your belongings, sprint out the door, and jump into the street every time your smoke detector goes off.

The first thing you do when the smoke detector goes off is you stop what you're doing. Then you look around to try to see what the actual problem is. Then, if it's a false alarm, you try to clear out the smoke to make the alarm turn off. You would never run out into the street, but you would also never try to go about your day without turning the alarm off. That would make any normal person go insane to try to continue cooking, cleaning, relaxing, and going to bed with the alarm still going off.

And yet, that's what most people are trying to do with their goals. They are trying to fight through their internal alarm, which just creates more friction and more frustration and leads to thoughts of feeling fake. I grew up in a very religious house where our church services were incredibly charismatic. We thought the way to reach God was to have as emotional of an experience as possible. When everyone could "feel" something, we liked to say that it was the presence of God. While there might be some truth to this, it was also an incredibly dangerous thing to do with our emotions. Knowing what I know now about our mind and emotions, what we were actually doing was training ourselves to believe that feelings equaled God. And no feelings meant no God, and lots of feelings meant lots of God.

This got me into a mental and emotional disaster in my teenage years, when I decided to go all in on this lifestyle and was determined to find God's will for my life. I thought I was seeking God, but really, I was seeking emotions. I could hardly decide what to wear to school without trying to feel for some type of voice or nudge from God. It got so bad that I stopped doing anything that brought me joy because the most powerful feelings I had happened to be negative and fear-based. As a result, my feelings, which I interpreted as God, told me to stop having fun and stop hanging out with people and, as a result, I had a mental breakdown without even knowing it.

The biggest danger of being led by feelings is that feelings go up and down. They are never constant or steady, and the only way to have success is to become someone who is constant and steady with your routines.

All of this makes our subconscious mind sound like a very negative thing. So why in the world do we have one? Well, the good news is that, with time and the right tools, you can actually retrain your mind for performance toward something you really want.

You see, your subconscious mind protects you, but as I also said, it automates your life by taking over tasks that no longer need your attention. Imagine if you could train it to perform the tasks that would lead you closer to your dreams instead of running away from them.

So, how do we reprogram our mindset? Well, let's talk about how our subconscious mind got its information in the first place. Our subconscious mind is a storing place for all of the things we have entered into our conscious minds. Our conscious minds are gathering information through our five senses. While you are reading this book right now, you are all at once feeling, tasting, smelling, seeing, and hearing. And those experiences are being collected as data about how the world works.

This is why your environment can be so dangerous. Someone who grows up surrounded by violence has trained their mind that the world is dangerous. It makes it ten times harder to trust people and believe in a better life. So much energy is put into survival that dreaming of something better becomes very hard. This, by the way, is why all of us should be more open to the idea of supporting people who come from different backgrounds. Never assume that success is just as easy for someone else just because they have access to the same internet you do. On one hand, you have to take ownership for where you are, but please don't judge others based on where they are. You have no idea what they had to go through just to make it to today.

Over time, your beliefs begin to be made up of the repetitions and emotional experiences you have. If something happens over and over, such as violence, your subconscious stores it away and performs it for you. If you are told over and over that you are stupid, then your subconscious takes over and performs that for you. Or if you have some type of emotional experience, such as being abused, in one event it can penetrate your subconscious and become a new belief. It seems unfair, but there is another side to this.

Positivity can be created through these same processes. If you repeat something positive over and over, or have an incredibly emotional positive experience, it can penetrate your beliefs and create a new one that now performs positive things by default. This is one of the reasons the rich get richer and the poor get poorer. People who have established thoughts of wealth and opportunity pass those beliefs on to their children, and those who struggle with poverty pass those thoughts on to their kids. This becomes what some would call a generational curse.

If you are like me, retraining your mind can be a very difficult task. But knowing what it would pass off to my kids by default was always my greatest motivation. My parents had passed poverty and lack to me by default, and I knew if I didn't do something to change it, my kids would end up with the same struggles I was having. Please remember that this process is 100 percent possible for everyone, but please don't assume that thirty years of beliefs will be rewritten in thirty days.

People who say a habit can be formed in thirty days start to sound really silly when you understand how your mind actually works. I always teach my clients that you can change your habits in thirty days, but in order to change your life, you have to continue your habits until they become new beliefs. This book is the start of your journey, but it can't be the end. When you are done reading this book, you need to read it at least two more times if you really want these beliefs to stick. I'm not saying that to make more sales, because you only have to pay once, and you already did that. I'm saying this because I want these things to stick.

What you really need to understand about your conscious mind is that it is just a free spirit looking around for something to experience. It isn't really positive or negative until you or your environment trains it to be. But once it is trained, it begins to see whatever it has been told to. If you teach it to see lack, it will find it everywhere it looks. And if you train it to see abundance, it will find that everywhere it looks. You will find the things you have been trained to see easily and naturally. And that's how success can eventually be easy.

Now let's talk about emotions, because these are what people often confuse with their hearts, which can completely derail any goal they have. Your emotions are just a chemical reaction to what your mind is saying. When your conscious mind receives a signal from your five senses, a flood of emotions is triggered throughout your body, telling it what to experience.

If you have eaten a donut before and it tasted amazing, the next time your body smells one, it will send a flood of emotions saying, "This is safe and makes me happy." From now on, you will love the smell of donuts. But in the same way, if you eat a food and it makes you sick, the smell or sight of that food from now on will cause a chemical reaction that tells you to run away.

While these feelings were created to protect you, they don't always do their job. The main reason is that your emotions are programmed based on how they will hurt or help *now*, not in the future. The biggest problem with this is that most things that comfort you right now can be detrimental to your future, and things that are good for your future often feel like pain and discomfort now.

So, your emotions can make it really easy to keep eating unhealthy foods, to keep watching Netflix instead of reading a book, and to keep scrolling on your phone when you should be working on your side hustle. This is another reason we have to be aware of all of this, so we can understand what is happening on the inside of us. Instead of thinking, *This is just so hard, it must not be what I'm supposed to do,* you can instead think, *These are just emotions trying to keep me comfortable in the present, but I want to do more things that take care of my future.*

Being aware is always the first step to growth because, without awareness, it's almost impossible to know what you should even work on. According to Carl Jung, "Until you make the unconscious conscious, it will rule your life and you will call it fate." What this means is that the things you are unconsciously creating will keep manifesting by default in your life. And your ignorance will naturally assume it must be fate, God, or the Universe that just didn't want it for you. You might start to think that you are actually destined to fail at business, to be out of shape, to be poor, or to be unhappy.

I found myself in my twenties trying to do new things, such as starting a business on the side and getting back in shape. But the negative emotions were so strong that I assumed it must be God telling me I was on the wrong path. The reality is it was just a poorly trained subconscious mind. What's crazy is that during that time I found a way to learn three different instruments, just because I wanted to so bad. I also figured out how to work ruthless days detailing cars in 100-degree heat, simply because I needed it so bad.

So, how do we fix all of this? How do we go about doing the work it takes to have new thoughts, beliefs, and feelings that serve us instead of slowly killing us? We learn how to find the voice of our heart.

If our heart is our constant connection to infinite wisdom, strength, and creativity, doesn't it make sense that the answers to our problems would already be on the inside? We just have to know how to listen.

I'm going to teach you the easiest way to find this voice, and then we'll talk about how to use this voice to realign your beliefs, feelings, and actions.

If the voice of our mind is based on past experiences, feelings, and failures, it is basically an internal documentary on all of our doubts, fears, insecurities, and failures. In other words, the voice of our head is rooted in doubt and lack. It is only seeing our lack of experience and strength and, therefore, seeing a lack of our ability to perform the new task.

The voice of our heart is not based on our past or anything else this earth knows. The voice of our heart is based on our future potential. Our heart is constantly seeing what we are capable of in the future, not what we may have failed at in the past. The voice of our heart comes in the form of our strength, abilities, purpose, potential, and faith. If your head is speaking from doubt and lack, your heart is speaking from faith and abundance. (See the image below for a visual of Head vs. Heart. I'll be referring to this chart throughout the book.)

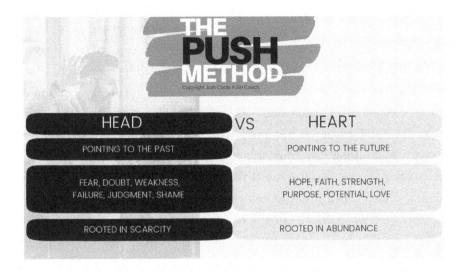

The best way to start the process of becoming the best version of yourself is to measure every single thought and ask if it's coming from doubt and lack or faith and abundance. The voice of lack might say that you've tried to get your business off the ground twenty times and always failed, so why would it work this time? But the voice of abundance might say that every day is another opportunity to create something new.

One of the greatest tricks to coaching yourself is to simply ask what advice you would give to someone else. Giving advice to others is so easy because you don't see all of their shortcomings the way you do when you look in the mirror. You don't judge them based on their past attempts or their lack of commitment. You only judge them based on what is possible.

If you ever struggle to find out what the voice of your heart is, try this trick I use on myself all the time. Simply ask yourself, *What does my Creator say about my purpose and my potential?* Something about envisioning our Creator almost immediately opens us up to our infinite connection. Even when working with people who had negative beliefs that came from religion, I've found that the second I ask them what their Creator would say, they are instantly able to see through the judgment and rules of humans and see a clear picture of a loving Creator.

Please remember that while religion can be a very positive thing, it is never a positive thing to allow the voices of other humans to outweigh the voice that lives inside us. If 99 percent of people are completely unaware of their subconscious mind, then please remember that even the best of people who may claim to represent God are still going to speak from their own doubts and fears on a pretty regular basis. Even if they are speaking from a Scripture that you hold dear to your belief system, they will still see that text through the lens of their own past and experiences. It is so important for you to understand this because I have found that religious ties can be the hardest thing to break. If you can convince yourself that the thing you're trying to do goes against your Creator, it will make it almost impossible to do. So, you have to be very careful to know that religion can be a wonderful thing if you don't allow the people who run the religion to replace the Creator it was meant to serve.

The same is true of your family. Your family might love you and genuinely care about you and your future. But please remember that by default, the only thing humans do is try to protect themselves, and their main way of doing this is by running away from anything that is uncomfortable. If you pursue something they don't understand, their first response will be to encourage you to run away. If that doesn't work, they will go to work, unconsciously, trying to save you by degrading you and humiliating you. Your friends and family might not even know they are doing it. They may think it's just fun and games. But they are unconsciously living their lives for safety and, therefore, unconsciously trying to sabotage anything in your life that threatens that safety they desire.

CREATING "BECAUSE" AFFIRMATIONS

Now that you know what's happening, let's talk about how to change it! One of the quotes I have coined over time says that "our limiting beliefs are constantly looking for a story to justify our fears and excuses." What this means is that once a belief settles into our subconscious, we start looking for proof of that belief, to turn it into a story we can stand behind. If you have convinced yourself that only outgoing people can have success, you'll follow all of the most outgoing people on Instagram and use that as your ongoing proof that introverts can't have success. You'll follow them religiously and be constantly triggered by their actions. As you see them traveling and speaking onstage, you'll just keep tallying up reasons you'll never be successful. Meanwhile, you'll somehow overlook the fact that 90 percent of successful online entrepreneurs are introverted. For most of them, that's why they decided to build a business online instead of in person.

I have always said that 90 percent of my most successful clients are introverts. The reason you thought they were so extroverted is because you saw them speaking onstage with confidence or hosting a call with a ton of energy. What you didn't see was how much time they put into working on their confidence and practicing public speaking and how they had to go pass out in a hotel room as soon as they were done speaking at the event.

The first step is just being aware of what excuses you are making. Take a minute to ask yourself, *What is the number one reason I'm telling myself that I can't be successful?* Write it down, no matter how silly it seems. The next thing is to ask yourself: *Is this based on my past fears and scarcity or on my future hopes, faith, and abundance?* I want you to actually write down next to the sentence you wrote, in all caps: "THIS IS BASED ON MY PAST FEARS AND SCARCITY; THEREFORE, IT IS NOT MY DESTINY."

Now you might feel fake going through this process, so let me remind you that what I'm about to teach you is not about whether you're telling the truth or lying. Please remember that there is a difference between truth and fact. A fact means that it is the current reality. A truth means that it is eternal. Based on that, your brain might be notifying you of current facts, but please remember that the truth can only be determined by eternal wisdom, which comes from the voice of your heart.

The next step is to ask yourself, *What does my Creator say about my potential to do this thing I want to do?* Write it down! I love this exercise because we all come from different backgrounds and belief systems, but asking this question forces us to find our deepest version of truth. Something about asking this question makes you go deeper than what others have told you or what lies you may have told yourself subconsciously to stay safe.

Now we take this new Heart Statement (or Creator Statement, if you prefer) and turn it into something we will say over and over until repetition trains us to bring up this thought by default instead of our old one.

If you say, "My Creator says I can do all things through his strength," your new Heart Statement might say, "Because I can do all things through my Creator's strength, I can build a successful business. In fact, I can do anything that is needed to create a successful business. That means I can go live on social media if that's what it takes. I can post incredible stories that connect to my ideal clients, and I can lead a team full of badasses. Because if I can do anything, there is not one single thing on my to-do list that I can't do."

You see, your brain is smart enough to know that the world works off of cause and effect. The reason your mind is looking for a story to justify your fears and excuses is so that it can logically say something like *"Because I am an introvert, I will never be successful"* or *"Because everyone who has success is extroverted, I will never be successful."*

The only true way to reprogram your brain is to find a new logical way to explain what you can have. Positive emotions do not fight negative emotions. That is why affirmations like "I'm a badass" or "I'm going to be healthy and successful" don't work, because you'll keep finding the old evidence and keep manifesting the old story.

The goal is to not get rid of the negative emotions as much as it is to retrain the underlying beliefs that tell us what to feel. If you can fix the beliefs, all of a sudden, those beliefs will send new signals of emotions that will help you succeed instead of holding you back.

These "because" affirmations are one of the main things that separate my system from that of other life coaches. I have learned from many other life coaches who teach you how to find the root of your problem but then just leave you there. It's almost like a doctor diagnosing you with a disease and then saying, "Well, now that you know, it will all be fine, right?"

I will admit that one of the most discouraging things in life can be to know that you are sick and not know why. There is definitely something about finally having a diagnosis that gives you a sense of freedom. But the only reason it gives you that sense is because you feel like you finally know what problem to address. You feel more confidence in finding a cure once you know what the issue is.

Life coaches, for some reason, have wrongfully assumed that awareness equals the cure. And to be perfectly honest, I don't even remember when or where I developed the idea for these action-based affirmations. Maybe it's because I'm an incredibly action-oriented person. I'm not the kind of person who can just be ok with the world having problems. Once I find out there is a problem, I just want to go to work to fix it. I'm the kind of person who is willing to do whatever work it takes if you'll just tell me what that work is.

That's one of the main reasons I decided to launch my own Life Coach Certification program last year. I wanted to teach a coaching system that is based on traditional coaching, which is diving into your head and finding the root of the issue, but added my PUSH Coach element, which is creating affirmations and an action plan to fix the problem.

So, while I want you to take the time to find the voice of your head and make sure you become aware of the disease that is trying to live on the inside of you, I'm begging you to not stop there. Please make sure you take the next step to creating your own cure through affirmations and writing the future that you really want!

COACHING QUESTIONS:

1. What is a goal you have been working toward or have wanted to work toward?

2. What have the voices of doubt tried to tell you about your goals?

3. If someone else came to you with this same limiting belief, what advice would you give them?

4. What do you believe your Creator would have to say about your limiting beliefs?

5. Fill in the blank: Because _____(the advice you would give someone else), I am more than capable of _____ (fill in the blank with your goal).

PS: If you want help setting your goals and/ or finding out if you're ready to coach others, you can go to https://www.joshcoats.com/survey to find out more about yourself. My team will also send you a free training to get you customized help for where you're at on your success journey!

3

TRUE COACHING

Social media has turned everyone into a "coach." And while I'm not completely against that, I want to take some time to teach you what true coaching really is. There is an idea of coaching that has been taken from the sports world. This version of coaching is a combination of people who have experience in a certain field, such as someone who used to play or someone who has a good mind for the sport. You have some people who were never good at the sport itself, but they're really good at motivating others who have more skill.

That's not the kind of coaching I want to talk about in this book. When I say that I want to teach you how to coach yourself and others to the next level of success, I'm not talking about looking in the mirror and saying positive things like "I am a badass!" and "I can be anything I want!" I am not talking about getting people on a call and telling them what worked for you. I am talking about *true* coaching, which is a process that I learned in my life coach training.

I always joke that life coaching is the mystical unicorn of the online world. The word "coach" is thrown around so much that people have kind of created their own meanings for it, but those of us who are trained in the true art of life coaching know the difference. It would be like the word "ninja" becoming a common word. What if everyone who had ever taken a karate class started calling themselves a "ninja"?

What if you logged into social media one day and your feed was filled with thousands of people who were calling themselves "ninjas"? What if they all started taking different specialties, so you had security ninjas, help-with-the-local-bully ninjas, birthday party ninjas, daytime ninjas, and so on? Those who were actually trained to be ninjas would feel very insulted.

I want to be clear: I'm totally fine with you calling yourself a life insurance coach, a health coach, a spiritual coach, or whatever you consider yourself. But most of the coaching genre is actually people who are consultants. Consultants speak from what they have personally experienced. I do a lot of consulting, so I don't have any issues whatsoever with consultants. But it's not coaching.

True coaching is the art of using questions to help others find their own heart voice. True coaching trusts that everyone else already has the answers they need. My job in coaching is not to bring an answer but instead to bring a lot of curiosity and questions. I'm like a detective trying to get to the bottom of the story so we can solve the case. But I wasn't an eyewitness to the crime, so I can't make up a story about what did or didn't happen. I have to interview others and get their perspectives.

Let me give you an example. I got a text from an old client. Amanda (name has been changed to protect my client) said, "Josh, I need your help. My ads aren't working anymore, and I need to figure out how to fix my sales."

We got on our first call, and she said, "Josh, I spend so much time mentoring others and helping them, and I feel like I need someone like you to just tell me what to do."

I reminded her, "Well, that's not what I'm going to do. You hired me to coach you, so that's what I'm going to do. I trust that you already have all of the answers. You have made millions of dollars because you are so smart and creative! I'm here to ask the questions, and I promise you that, with enough of the right questions, the answer will present itself!"

This isn't really anyone's favorite thing to hear. People would much rather me say something like "Don't worry, I have three secrets to 10X-ing your sales and, if you just follow these three things that no one else has ever heard of, it will work overnight like it did for me!"

There are a few problems with this approach.

First, nothing has ever worked for me overnight. Even things that looked like they happened overnight were the result of several years of building up to that overnight success. My first book became a number one best seller in an hour, but that was after five years of networking, posting, doing monthly free calls, and training tens of thousands of people. I guess I could put together a "How to become a best seller in less than an hour," but you would be very disappointed to see just how many things you would have to do to get to that point.

Second, this approach is dangerous because no one else can do exactly what you have done and get the same results. Think about it: not only are they on a different timeline but they also have different skill sets, different schedules, different resources, and of course different beliefs about what they can and can't do.

So, I dug into some questions with Amanda. After she gave me the back-story to what was going on and shared her frustrations, I just asked, "What are all of the ways that worked before you ever used paid advertising?"

Sometimes I find that clients evolve into something new and tend to leave behind other things that aren't as popular but still work just as well. She started listing some things. As she said them out loud, she realized that she had stopped doing some of these things. Step one: let's do those things again!

Then I dug deeper. We can't just bring up the past. We have to always look to the future and ask if there are better ways. That's why Amanda decided to start using paid advertising.

So, let's see if there are some other new ideas in there! I asked her, "What are all of the ways you can think of that could increase your sales?"

She sat and thought for a minute. She spewed out a few ideas. And then I saw it happen. I can always tell when people finally run out of head knowledge and, without realizing it, dig deeper into their heart for better information. You see, if you can ask enough questions, or just the right questions, your head has this moment where it finally says to your heart, "I'm out of ideas. Do you have anything?"

Remember, your heart is rooted in love. It is incapable of interrupting and trying to take control. Your heart is patiently waiting for that magical moment when the question is so good that your head gives up. That's when your heart steps in. The person it's happening to isn't always aware of it, but if you're listening and watching, you can see and feel it. You hear the excitement in their voice. You also notice the difference in their posture. The biggest tip for me is the words they choose. When the head voice is talking, we tend to say things like "I feel like ... " When the heart is speaking, we tend to say things like "I *know* that ... "

As Amanda rattled off random ideas—probably things she had heard others say—she eventually said, "I could speak on podcasts! I know a lot of people who have larger shows, and I know I would be great, and I know it would drive a ton of traffic with each episode."

She then tried to keep going and shared many more ideas. You'll notice that once the heart has an amazing idea, the head gets a little jealous and feels the need to throw out some ideas of its own. Your head is like the annoying friend who has to one-up everyone's stories with stories that annoy everyone in the room! But I heard her heart shine and, as she tried to move on, I stopped her.

"Wait, we have it!" I said.

She looked at me, confused. "What do you mean?" she asked.

Why in the world would she even ask? Didn't she see, hear, and feel her own excitement? Maybe. But this is why having a properly trained coach is so powerful. A few things happen to us when we have our best ideas.

Sometimes we hear the idea, and in our heart, we know it's great. But we immediately calculate the work and responsibility attached to it and try to wave it off like it doesn't matter. We tend to downplay our own good ideas because we don't know if we really want to follow through on them.

We also tend to downplay our own ideas because we're still looking for someone else to solve our problems for us. We haven't learned to trust our own intuition. And that's why it's so important to learn true coaching. Whether it's coaching yourself or coaching others, this process teaches people to start trusting themselves. Amanda may have never used this idea if I hadn't been there to catch her and give her the proper credit for her own idea.

I said, "Amanda, did you hear yourself? You have been throwing out ideas left and right. With every idea, you have sounded like a zombie muttering off random data or maybe some type of computer code you don't even understand. And then your eyes lit up and you said, with so much confidence, 'I know it would drive a ton of traffic with each episode.'"

I then explained the head voice versus the heart voice to her. I could tell she was so relieved to not only have a solid idea for us to build on but also see that her money invested in a professional "question asker" was going to pay off.

From there, the questions just kept digging. "Who could you reach out to? What could we say to them? What is something you could give away for free to make sure their listeners follow through on seeking you out?"

One hour later, we had a master plan for getting her business back on track. She sent me a voice message after our call and told me how amazing it felt to have a true coach back in her life. She explained that she had worked with a lot of agencies and consultants over the past several years. While some of those services had helped her business, none of them had made her feel truly supported in her power.

Dear consultants, it's ok if you want to share your experiences and give advice based on things that have worked for you, but *please* also learn how to coach. Learn how to ask questions and help others find their power. Fixing someone's traffic or engagement, helping someone lose fifteen pounds, or teaching someone how to start a DIY project might fix their current pain. But true coaching is all about helping people find their own power. That is something that will pay off over and over again.

I am constantly teaching the leaders in my group that if they can gain confidence, momentum, and the right energy, they can do anything they want with their lives and businesses. But if you don't have confidence, energy, or momentum, all of the right strategies, sales pages, and engagement won't even matter. A person who doesn't understand their own power is helpless, even if they have a million dollars in their bank account.

So, let's talk about a few of my favorite coaching techniques. And as you read the rest of this book, you'll find some coaching questions around the content I'm teaching. I want to be careful to teach you some principles and then give you questions to ask yourself and others on how to implement them in your life and circumstances. You may find that I tend to relate everything to business, but true personal growth always applies to all areas of life. So please remember to use the coaching questions to help you dig in and apply them to what needs your focus right now!

QUESTIONS THAT ENGAGE THE HEART

The biggest goal of coaching is to help others find their heart voice. Remember that your head is trying to see the world through scarcity. It is trying to keep you safe, which means it is bringing up the worst-case scenario for every decision you make. I would actually go a step further and say that it even exaggerates the worst-case scenario to make it sound worse than what it really is.

What we need to do is make sure we ask ourselves and others questions that use the different characteristics of the heart.

James asked me, "Josh, I really want to reach out to more people on social media, but it feels so fake. I don't want to be some salesy weirdo in someone's inbox."

I have had these same fears before. My second year in business, I was scared to death to reach out to people on social media and offer them a free coaching call. One woman who took me up on a free call ended up bringing up some marriage problems she was having. Her family was pressuring her to leave her husband because of some religious differences. She loved her husband. She didn't want to leave. But she also didn't want to let her family down. After some really deep questions about what *she* believed, she was able to put aside her family's opinions and find her own power. She was in tears as she felt the power to defy her family and make a marriage work. She said, "Josh, you have no idea how long I have been praying for someone to help me with this."

That day, coaching saved a marriage. Not me, because I didn't do it. I just asked the questions and trusted that she would find her power. I used this session as motivation to go talk to others. I found that was my purpose, which is one of the heart words, and my head fueled me to deal with some of the rejection that would come along with it.

"James," I asked, "what is it you would help these people with if you did get the courage to reach out?"

"Well," he said, pausing for a second as his head opted out and gave his heart permission to chime in, "I would help them. I would help them create a healthy life."

"And what would that do for them and their families?" I asked.

"They would feel more confident in their own skin. They would be able to play with their kids on the playground. They would create a new legacy as they pass off these new habits to their kids, who would pass them down to their kids."

He found it. James found his power! Now I just had to teach him how to hold onto it.

"So, if you don't reach out to any of these people, what will happen?" I asked.

"They won't get the help they need." He was now starting to tear up. "They'll be stuck like I was. They might miss out on memories with their family. They'll hide from the camera and always be on the sideline, watching their family instead of being there creating memories with them."

"So, what is more authentic?" I asked. "Being true to your purpose of helping others or being true to your feelings of worrying about what others will think of you?"

The next step I take is making sure I help them turn their own heart words into an affirmation. I don't want to make an affirmation for them from my heart. It has to be their own words that bring them to tears. The words that brought them to tears today are the same ones that will bring them to tears tomorrow and even a year from now.

Here's the affirmation I would give this person: Because I want to help others create a healthy life, where they feel confident in their own skin, can play with their kids on the playground, and create a legacy as they pass off these new habits to their kids and their grandkids and beyond, I am reaching out to every person I can find to offer them this life-changing opportunity!

I assign them to say this affirmation every morning and evening and right before they send any messages for the day. It will be weird at first, but this is how we embrace the heart first. This same process can be followed by someone who is wanting to lose weight or get healthier. Ask yourself, *What is the purpose? Who will this affect? And if I don't follow through, how will it hurt myself and others?*

Whatever your answer is, that's the affirmation followed by what it is you're going to actually do. If you need extra motivation to read more books, ask yourself, *What will reading do for my personal life and career? How will it move my purpose and mission forward even faster? Who will it have an impact on?*

I have found that most of us are willing to do for others more than we will do for ourselves. If I can point myself and others to purpose, I can usually coach someone into finding their heart voice and finding a deeper level of motivation.

In the same way I used purpose, you can grab any of the heart words from my Head vs. Heart graphic, or other heart words you find along the way.

If you know someone has a background in faith, it can be a powerful thing to bring faith into the situation. Just be careful to not bring up words that might trigger the head voice. For example, if you ask someone, "What would your church think or say about that?" it might cause people to go into their head to look for past things that have been said that may be healthy or might not be healthy at all. Not everything that is said by people who go to church is good. They are just people who, like everyone else, might be talking from their head instead of their heart.

I would ask them instead, "What do you believe your Creator would say about that?" You see, there's something about bypassing human opinions and going straight to our Creator that causes us to think from our heart and let go of the opinions of others.

One of my other favorite coaching questions is this simple: "Are you trying to choose 'or' instead of 'and'?"

"Josh, I really want to grow my business, but I'm not trying to be one of those moms who works all day and night," Jessica told me.

She was a little snarky about it, and I could tell she had a little superiority complex toward people who work a lot.

"Well, Jessica, what would it look like to grow your business *and* be a great mom?"

"I mean, I just see all of these moms who post all day and night on social media and there's no way they are spending any quality time with their kids," she told me, still a little snarky.

"Can I ask you something, Jessica?" I asked as I prepared my next question with caution, knowing that she was already a little triggered. "Why are you choosing 'or' instead of 'and'?"

"What do you mean?" she asked, a little offended. "I just want to be an amazing mom."

Here's where I dug a little deeper with the purpose button.

"What do you want for your kids' future? What do you want them to grow up to be?"

Jessica got very proud as she explained, "I want them to be anything they want to be. I want my little boy to grow up and be an astronaut if he wants. I want my girl to be the first female president if she wants." (I'm praying this dates this book sooner rather than later.)

"Ok, so here's another question for you," I said, hoping she was ready for some tough love. "If you want your kids to be anything in the world they want to be, why would you, their greatest example of what life should look like, do anything less?"

The Zoom room went quiet. And then there were tears. And then she finally explained on a deeper level, for the first time, without any judgment toward others in her voice. "I know I need to step up my game. I know I have more in me. It's just that I love my work so much that I don't know how to check out. So, I find that it's safer to just not let myself dream anymore. If I dream too big, I'll just fall back into being a bad mom."

Jessica wasn't really upset at other moms who work too much. She was mad at herself for all of the times she worked too much.

"What if we stop trying to be the most successful entrepreneur *or* the best mom and just decide to be the most successful entrepreneur *and* the best mom? What if we create boundaries for your business and find a creative way to grow like never before but *only* inside very specific boundaries to protect your time *and* energy that you want to have for your kids?"

Jessica finally gave in. "I would love that," she said with relief.

Jessica found her power that day. We created a strict schedule. She had to text me every day at 4 pm to tell me she was clocking out and taking her kids to the park. And the really cool thing was that her business grew as she finally understood that working less forced her to focus more on what mattered and let go of what didn't matter. She outsourced parts of her business that didn't need her attention. She marked things off of her to-do list that weren't moving her business forward. She had new creative ideas as she was forced to ask herself regularly, *How could I motivate others to show up in less time? How could I produce more results in less time?*

I trust that Jessica is still finding new ways even today to continue growing faster and faster without sacrificing any precious memories with those two kids.

True coaching is the art of asking intentional questions that force yourself and others to look at things in a way they've never looked at them before. We have been trained and programmed to live life based on the voices and experiences of the past. The biggest problem with this is that the voices we have listened to were those that weren't trained to find their heart voices.

A lot of really good people have given a lot of really bad advice. Some of these people have had titles that made us think they were smarter than they really were. Coaches, teachers, and pastors with good intentions have led a lot of people astray with voices of doubt and scarcity.

We now have thousands of years of bad advice being passed down. Very few people have taken the time to stop and ask, "Is this really in alignment with what I really believe about life? About success? About my Creator? About me?"

Coaching is the single greatest gift that was ever given to me, which is why I launched my own Life Coach Certification program in 2021. Coming out of a world pandemic that may or may not be over by the time this book is published, I had spent seven years coaching others and helping them find their power, but I knew it was time for the next evolution. I knew it was time for me to pass on the art, not just the experience. It's a wonderful thing when I can coach someone else, but how much more powerful could it be if I trained others to coach?

What would happen if we had an army of people who wanted to help others truly find their power, teach them things that would help them for a season, share a few principles on growth, or give them a guideline to success. And then, actually teach them to use the most universal leadership tool on the planet whose purpose is to help others find their heart voice, where infinite wisdom, creativity, and intelligence is just waiting to be called on?

If you want to learn more about joining this army, shoot me an email at info@joshcoats.com or check out my resources at www.joshcoats.com.

This book is the first of many resources to come for people who want to learn how to really think differently. I have created so many resources on how to sell more, how to lead better, and so many other business-related topics. But this book will teach you how to think better so that you can approach anything and everything that life or business may demand of you.

When you know how to coach yourself, you can find yourself in any situation and know how to get the answers you need. You will understand that the answers are not on the outside somewhere. The answers are not on social media, and they definitely aren't in the news. The most important answers you will ever get will come from the inside.

As you learn to coach yourself through life and business, you will also know how to coach others—not because you have all of the answers but because you have learned to trust the answers they have living on the inside.

This book is a collection of all of the things I have coached myself through to build a seven-figure coaching business. But don't let that fool you into thinking these lessons only apply to business. The reality is, the person who seeks out their very best self will be equipped for anything life brings.

The person who is motivated by personal growth instead of personal gain will always have everything they want in life. The person who is motivated by personal gain instead of personal growth may get everything they want on the outside, but they will never find fulfillment on the inside.

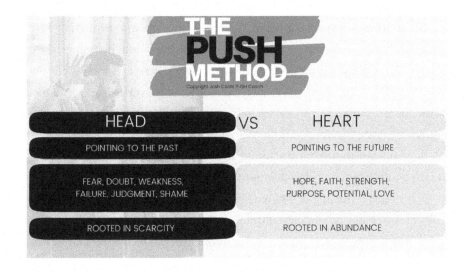

COACHING QUESTIONS

1. What is the difference between coaching and consulting?

2. Why do you think most people would rather be told what to do than get true coaching that digs into their own power and beliefs?

3. When the head voice is talking we tend to say things like _____ , when the heart voice is talking we tend to say things like _____.

4. When you think about the goal you are currently working toward, what are some things you "feel" vs some things you KNOW?

5. What are some things that used to work for you, that you might have abandoned too soon, that could still serve you in your pursuit for the next level of success?

6. When you think about your next big goal, what are some ways you can tie your purpose to it so that it doesn't feel selfish or vain?

7. What are some boundaries you can put into place to protect your personal life from the pursuit of your next goal? How can you make this an AND situation? Example: I'm going to _____ (insert your goal) while also maintaining _____ (insert something in your personal life you refuse to lose in the process).

Are you falling in love with the idea and process of coaching? If you think you might want to learn more about coaching yourself and others, just go to https://www.joshcoats.com/survey to find out if you're ready to step into the role of a coach!

4

THE MOTIVATION HACK

Your quest to find the best version of you will come with many obstacles. And even after you learn how to find your heart voice and start to implement what I've taught you about affirmations, you will run into this recurring problem: motivation.

Motivation has got to be one of the number one reasons people give for not taking on the next chapter of their lives. That word sometimes comes out as "This doesn't feel authentic" or "I need more balance in my life," but really people are saying over and over that they don't have the right *feelings* to make the changes they want to make.

We as a society have been tricked into thinking things have to feel a certain way. We buy into this lie because, at the end of the day, we all want to feel good.

So I want to teach you the greatest motivation hack that exists. While motivation is not the one single thing that creates success, I don't know of anyone who has created success in any area of their life without it. While there are many different things you need to learn and implement, all of them will take a high level of motivation. So many people think that there are naturally motivated people who just wake up full of life and energy. If you are someone who doesn't have that natural level of motivation, you might feel like you don't stand a chance. That is just not true.

The most important thing you will ever learn about motivation is simply this: motivation is a *gimmick*. It's not even real. Motivation is this idea that if you can somehow manipulate outward circumstances and find a way to *feel* good, you could finally *do* good. Here's the problem with that: the outward circumstances are ever-changing. One day it's sunny, the next day it's cloudy. If you live in Tulsa like me, it may rain and shine on the same day and then a tornado might hit.

You will have days when all of your feelings align and help you produce a ton of progress. But success isn't about conquering one day here and one day there. Success is found in the routines you create and sustain day after day. If you constantly depend on outward things, you will never have total control over your life. And one of the keys to getting what you want is taking full responsibility and full control of all the things you can control.

I have found that motivation is no longer needed when you have something more powerful, and I call it "inspiration." Motivation comes from the outside, so it's not reliable and definitely not predictable. But like everything else I'm teaching you in this book, inspiration comes from the inside. I want to teach you the two ways you can find that inspiration anytime you need it.

1. Life Vision

One of the greatest lessons life coaching taught me is to approach every situation by starting with the end in mind. Most people live their lives in a reactive state. Even when they have goals, those goals are based on what they think they should do, based on society or something they saw on Instagram. When you are proactive, you take time to go inward and ask this question: *What do I really want in life?*

When you imagine yourself ten years down the road, what do you want to be doing? If you have a family, like me, ask what kind of a life you want to give to your loved ones. Take five minutes and answer these questions. No, really, answer these questions:

In a perfect life, where do you see yourself living?
What kinds of vacations and trips do you take?
What kind of health do you have?
What kind of money do you make?
What are you doing for a living?

Now I want you to ask another powerful question: *Why* do you want these things?

I found myself at thirty years old having to ask my mom if she would buy my kids new clothes for school, because I couldn't afford to. Actually, that's a lie. I didn't ask. I was too embarrassed. Instead, I just sat and waited and hoped that she would notice. We built a house down the street from my parents' house and went to the same church every Sunday. Usually, about a week before school started, my mom would try to ask. My mom is the sweetest thing in the world. At 5'3", she worked a full-time job her whole life while cooking, cleaning, taking us to practice, and going to church three times a week. She didn't volunteer at church as often as my dad because she was usually the one who took care of me and my siblings.

My mom is the kind of person who will cook and clean all day and then iron our clothes for us before bed. She wouldn't complain one single time. She loved to give and serve. About a week before school, she would look at the kids and ask, in the sweetest voice, "Do you kids need some school clothes?" I would be embarrassed and make up an excuse about how I didn't have time or about getting paid the next week.

"That's ok," my mom would say. "I'll take them this weekend to get new clothes." Even though my parents didn't have a lot of money, they made enough to have a relaxed life and spent all of their extra money on their grandkids. My kids never went somewhere with my mom and came home empty-handed.

Here's the part I'm most embarrassed about. My kids would bring home birthday invitations from friends at school. I knew I couldn't afford to buy their friend a present, so to avoid the embarrassment of showing up as the only ones who didn't bring a gift, I would set the invitation on the counter. With three kids, I knew if I just put it there and paid no attention to it, it would either disappear or my kids would forget about it until it was too late.

If it wasn't bad enough that my kids didn't get to do fun things, they also had to miss out on the fun things that other parents were trying to pay for because I was too pathetic to have an extra $10 to buy a present.

Let me just take a second to say, I know these stories don't give you the best picture of me. When you write a book, you're really supposed to spend the whole book building yourself up and telling everyone how you are personal friends with Oprah and hang out with Coldplay on weekends.

The reality is I don't need you to finish this book and think I'm a rock star. I need you to finish this book and believe that *you* can be a rock star. If the only thing I accomplish with this book is making myself look famous and untouchable, I have failed both you and my Creator. I wrote this book because I had a message that was burning in my soul that I needed you to get a hold of. I don't need you to get a hold of my résumé; I need you to get a hold of my purpose and conviction. I need you to take extreme responsibility for your life and your potential.

When I began to picture the life I really wanted, I wasn't thinking about having a Mercedes-Benz or buying a mansion on the beach. I just wanted to create a life for my kids that allowed them to have the life experiences I knew they deserved. I wanted to create a life where I could bless them financially and be there as often as possible to create memories with them.

That's where it started for me. That was my superpower. When I took my business to social media in 2015, I messaged every single person on the planet and offered them one free call to see if I could help them with anything. Message after message, I felt stupid. I felt like a car salesman knocking on people's windows as they drove by. I felt like everyone on the other side of the message probably hated me for interrupting their day.

One day, I was trying to be really self-aware and thought to myself, *I think I have a problem caring too much about what people think of me.* I heard my kids playing on the other side of my office door and remembered what mattered. I realized, almost out loud, *I don't have a problem caring too much about what people think of me. I have a problem caring too much about what the wrong people think of me.*

Here I was, worried about some type of message thread being started about me while my kids were wearing old clothes and missing out on birthday parties. At that moment, I decided I would message every single person on the planet if it meant giving my kids a better life.

Once I'd learned how to visualize my ideal life and realize who it was attached to, I no longer needed motivation. I also never needed anyone else's permission or approval again. I became an unstoppable force! If you constantly find yourself needing someone else's approval or permission, you might need to take some time to reflect on who you are fighting for. And remember that the people you are fighting for are sometimes the same people who are criticizing you and trying to hold you back. But sometimes you have to remember that you are a #grownassadult. You didn't need their permission to like the shoes or Netflix show you like, so why do you need their permission to do what you believe is best for them, even if they haven't seen it yet?

If you struggle with what others think of you, please write this down somewhere near your computer: "Stop looking to others for the affirmation and confirmation you should have given yourself when you woke up this morning."

If you want to be a leader in any area of your life, you will have to learn to be your own biggest cheerleader. If you are someone like me who motivates or mentors others for a living, you will have to remember that it is not another person's job to motivate or support you. I see so many people online building businesses who are looking for their "tribe." The biggest problem with this is that they are asking others to pay money to be the support that they are needing for themselves. Don't go to social media to build the tribe you need. Go to social media to be the tribe others need. If you still need others to believe in you or encourage you, you shouldn't be charging them money. Go find a mentor if you need that.

2. LIFE MISSION

Your life vision is the thing that keeps you fighting for yourself and your loved ones, but if you don't combine it with your life mission, you run the risk of finding yourself feeling selfish and unfulfilled. You might also find yourself outgrowing your life vision and feeling like there's nothing left for you to do. Every time I teach on life vision at a retreat or workshop, there is one person who speaks up and says something like "What about me? I already have a lot of money and I'm content. I don't need anything else."

There are a few words that get me fired up with anger. One of them is "content." Somewhere, someone told us that being content was the most important thing in life. We use this word to try to make it sound like we aren't selfish because only a selfish person would have everything they need and still want more, right? I believe that the person who has everything they need and never takes the time to help others is the most selfish person in the world.

Saying you're content just means you got all of your dreams and forgot that the world around you is still in pain. Until there are no problems left in the world, there will always be more work to do. That is where the life mission comes in. Your life mission is the thing you feel compelled to fix in the world.

I'll never forget the day I was driving home in my Nissan Xterra from a day of detailing cars. I was thinking about the work I was doing in my new business as a life coach and had this conflicting excitement. On one hand, I was so excited about where I believed this journey would take me. On the other hand, I was frustrated at how slowly I was progressing. I said out loud to God, "I will do whatever I have to do to figure out this business thing and, when I do, I'll spend the rest of my life teaching others how to do the same."

That is still my biggest motivation for the many training courses I've put out and the reason I just recently launched my own Life Coach Certification program. I'm committed to being a cure for the thing that used to be my biggest pain.

I'm so desperately moved by the desperation in the world around me. I can't drive home from the coffee shop during rush hour without asking myself, *What are all of these people doing spending their mornings and evenings stuck in traffic to work at a job they hate?*

I can't go to a coffee shop without running into a local friend who is working on a side grind. It doesn't matter what project I have going on, I have to pause and give them some of my time. Whether it's an idea I can share with them or even just a hug and a reminder that they're on the same path, my mission is the blood flowing in my veins. The older I get, the more my mission matters and the less a lake house matters. The older I get, the more I want to give and the less I need to receive in advance.

I've recently been inspired by the intro of a book I read in an airport. It was talking about being a leader who connects. I would tell you the title of the book, but it was terrible. The intro changed my life, but I just couldn't get into anything else in the book. I will share with you the portion of the intro that challenged and changed me.

The idea was that leaders need to take initiative to connect with other leaders with no agenda. Leaders need to take the time to connect with people because they care, not because they want something in advance. I will admit that, over time, I have learned to protect my schedule. I wanted to protect my energy to make sure I could give my best to the people who earned it and have plenty left for my family. But I forgot something that I teach all the time. When you spend enough time with the right people, you don't lose time or energy. Time and energy are both multiplied when you surround yourself with the right people.

The last several weeks, I have been saying yes to anyone who is a person of influence. I've been going out of my way to connect with people who I know are making a difference in the world. I'm not connecting so that I can get into their circle. I'm not looking for a speaking opportunity. I am connecting because I know the power of leaders coming together. I am looking for a way to serve someone who I know is out there changing the world. I know that if I can encourage them, I will also be encouraged. I know that if I encourage them, they will encourage someone else.

During my meditation time in the pool this morning, I prayed out loud, "I am seeking out the people who are making a difference. I am connecting with leaders of leaders so that I can change the world by empowering other leaders."

As I'm writing this, I'm a few days away from a trip to Arizona. I'm traveling to Scottsdale, Arizona, to an event that is being put on by a company I work with. I'm not associated with the company, but many of the sales reps inside the company hire me for leadership training and life coaching. A few thousand of them will gather. Normally, I wouldn't go because I don't get an invite, but this year I was chatting with one of the top leaders and she was struggling big time. I asked how many people in her company were struggling with the same issue.

"All of them," she said.

"I'm coming," I said. I don't care if I have an invite, I'm getting an Airbnb and having several of them over to my house for a workshop. While I'm there, I'm inviting past clients to stop by for dinner. I feel in my soul that if I don't take massive action to recharge the leaders in this specific company, there could be some really rough days ahead. There is no worse scenario for the future of a company than for its leaders to lose hope and confidence. The leaders in this company have been very good to me. They have flown me across the country (and Canada too) to speak at events and retreats. They have opened many doors for me, and they will always have a special place in my heart. So, I'm committed to recharging them, and I don't need anything out of it.

I'm not going to Scottsdale to try to land a new client. I'm not going because it will look good on Instagram. I'm going because there are leaders who need me.

What is it that you are currently working toward in your life? Or maybe there's something you've already conquered that has created a passion inside of you? I once heard that when you find the thing in the world that brings tears to your eyes, you know you have found your conviction and your calling.

I grew up in a house that was religious to the extreme. To be clear, religion can be a very healthy thing, but when taken to the extreme, it can be very damaging. We had an obsession with what we called sin. We spent more time talking about what was a sin than we did talking about God's love. We overanalyzed everything in the world to try to find all of the things that were sinful so we could make sure to avoid them.

I don't use the word "sin" in my everyday vocabulary anymore, but there is one singular thing that I still see as a sin. The only way to "sin," in my opinion, is to find your calling and conviction and ignore it. There is a whole chapter on spirituality later in the book, but I wanted to go ahead and make this point now. Ignoring your calling is the fastest way to find yourself spiritually dead. And the quickest way to reignite your life from the inside out is to just say yes to that inner calling.

You might not know what it looks like to do the thing your heart is calling for, but it is your inner light, and it will guide the way for you. If you will just commit to following that purpose, it will open doors for you and lead you places you never thought possible. What a shame it would be to take up space on this planet for decades and never even give into the reason and purpose you were put here.

I tell my clients all the time that the day I can no longer add value to the world around me, I'm ready to get out of here. I enjoy Netflix, and there are some great movies out there. But the pain of this world isn't worth being here if the only thing you have to look forward to is the next episode of your favorite show. There is a world out there that needs your voice. Don't feel like you fit in? All the more reason the world needs you.

Are you the first in your family to try? Good, you can set a new trend. You can make the path easier for someone else. My mission started with making an easier path to success for my kids, but it then extended to everyone in the world who identifies with my story in any way.

Regardless of your background, religion, ethnicity, or sexual orientation, the world needs you to stand up proud and do what you do! If we're being real, the more different you feel you are, the *more* this world needs you. This world already has enough perfect and pretty people to look up to. I think it's about time we gave the world some new faces to look to.

If I had been born into wealth or graduated from Stanford or were a child prodigy, you might still read my story, but you wouldn't be as inspired. I bet the reason you are inspired by my story is because I'm a kid from

Haysville, Kansas, who found himself detailing cars and playing in rock bands on the weekend. We love to worship the stories of perfect people because it excuses us from trying. But we relate to the stories of imperfect people. John Maxwell says that if you want to impress someone, share your wins. But if you want to inspire someone, share your losses. It's time to stop using your past and weaknesses as an excuse. Decide today that your pain is your superpower!

COACHING QUESTIONS

1. The most important thing you will ever learn about motivation is simply this: motivation is a

_____

2. I have found that motivation is no longer needed when you have something more powerful, and I call it

_____

LIFE VISION COACHING QUESTIONS

This is just a starting place to get your brain working. If you want to learn more on how to coach yourself, make sure to check out my other resources at www.joshcoats.com.

1. Imagine your life five years from now. If you could have and do anything you want, what would it look like?

_____

_____

_____

2. What are a few goals you want to accomplish?

_____

_____

_____

3. What would you do for a living?

_____

_____

_____

4. What kind of money would you make per year?

_____

_____

_____

5. What kind of life experiences would you be able to give your loved ones?

_____

_____

_____

6. How would this new life make you feel?

_____

_____

_____

7. How would this new life impact your legacy?

_____

_____

_____

LIFE MISSION COACHING QUESTIONS

1. What is a specific thing in the world that breaks your heart when you see it and compels you to take action?

_____

_____

_____

2. What is something you have personally struggled with that you had to work to overcome?

_____

_____

_____

3. What are some "power" adjectives that you think of when you think of yourself (i.e., strong, courageous, energetic, steady, bold, calm)?

_____

_____

_____

4. Can you put some of these ideas into a simple one- to two-sentence mission statement that says who you are and what you want to give to the world?

_____

_____

_____

Here's my personal mission statement as an example: I am an energetic force of light, pushing entrepreneurs to reach their full potential.

Need help with your mission statement? Try asking four or five friends what positive adjectives they think of when they think of you. Sometimes others have better words for us than we do!

5

GETTING THE UNIVERSE
ON YOUR SIDE

I believe that there are principles that govern our Universe that were put here to help us and protect us, but most people never learn how to use them, so it starts to feel like the Universe is against us. Once you learn how these principles work, you start to realize just how simple it is to get the things you really want in life.

I want to share the two principles that I believe are the core principles of the entire planet. Use them properly, and they will change your life forever. Ignore them, and you will make life one hundred times harder than it needs to be.

The first is the Law of Sowing and Reaping. This one is pretty simple. It says that what you sow is what you will reap. While this principle sounds underwhelmingly basic, there is a reason most people never take advantage of it. Almost everyone underestimates the amount of time it takes your seed to turn into a harvest.

I want you to take a second to close your eyes and visualize a flower. Imagine the most beautiful flower in the world. Pause for five seconds and think about it.

Tell me this, did you imagine the part of the flower that is above ground or underground? I've used this analogy since the very first event I ever put on. Only eight people were in attendance, and I didn't have proof of my analogy yet, but it was the thing that I was reminding myself of daily as I patiently waited for my flower to bloom. Using this analogy over and over, more than 95 percent of people admit that the only part of the flower they had imagined was the part above ground. No one really considers what had to exist below ground because that wasn't the end goal people were going for.

When we plant a flower seed, that seed is the flower. It contains everything that will ever be needed right inside. But you would never plant that seed in the ground and then run over to your neighbor and start jumping and screaming, "Look, I have a beautiful flower. It's my favorite one." If you did, your neighbor might never invite you over again, or they might ask who your dealer is and what kind of prices you get.

When you plant that seed, you know that you have a flower, but you still don't have what you really want. So, you water it and make sure it gets enough sunshine. And you wait patiently. After a few days you might get a little stem popping up, and once again you could technically run over to your neighbor and say, "Look, I have a flower!" He wouldn't be impressed. This is your first sign of outward proof, but it's still not what you want.

You have to keep watering and protecting your seed until you eventually get what you want. You have to be very careful during this process not to get too frustrated by the rate of growth and just trust that one day you will have what you really want. You also have to be very careful not to compare your flower to someone else's who may have planted their flower long before you. We tend to compare the flowers we planted yesterday to the flowers someone else planted months ago. And then we think there's something wrong with our flowers or something wrong with us.

The flower analogy is how our goals work. You might have the greatest idea in the world for a new business, or maybe even just a new idea for your current business. I need you to understand that you are the seed, and you already have everything you will ever need living on the inside. But you will have to water that seed, give it light, and protect it. If you do, it will start to grow a little. But even when it does grow, you have to be very careful not to compare your one-month progress to someone else's ten-year progress. I also want you to remember that some flowers take a lot longer to grow and bloom than others. So don't compare your dream or journey to anyone else's timeline. The person who has ten pounds to lose may only need a few months to hit their goal weight. The person who needs to lose one hundred pounds will not reach their goal as fast as the person who only needs to lose ten. That doesn't mean that the person with one hundred pounds can't reach their goal; it just means they have a different timeline.

Comparison is one of the biggest threats to your success. I was just telling one of my groups today that you have to train yourself to see the world through abundance. It is your head voice, the voice of scarcity, that wants to see the success of others and use it as an excuse for why you can't do it. If they have more followers, scarcity says that it's not fair because you don't have as many followers, so the same thing could never work for you. Scarcity will always make an excuse for why you can't do what someone else can do.

Abundance will look at someone else's success and thank them for paving a path for you. Abundance will see that there is something you can learn from them even if you're not on the exact same path.

I found myself looking at someone's post today on Instagram. It had ten times the number of likes as my posts. I immediately thought, *This is ridiculous. This post isn't even very good. I say better things than this all the time.*

And then I stopped and asked myself, *Have you done everything he has done to have as many fans as him?*

And then I realized that jealousy was causing me to criticize this person. This was feeding negative emotions. Even worse, I realized that I couldn't possibly learn from this person and judge them at the same time. Here was someone who was doing things on the level I wanted to be on and, instead of learning from him, my jealousy and ego were blocking me from the very lessons that could have got me to the place I wanted to go.

The only way you don't get what you want in life is if you stop believing in the process and stop protecting your seed. The Law of Sowing and Reaping really should be called the Law of Sowing and Waiting.

Please remember that your goal has nothing to do with your worth or whether or not you are good enough. The Law of Sowing and Reaping says that anyone who sows the seed and gives it water and light will get a harvest. Imagine someone thinking they aren't worthy of getting a flower to grow? Doesn't that sound ridiculous? And yet people say it about growing a business all the time. People say it about why they can't lose weight all the time.

There are a ton of assholes in this world who make a ton of money. Why is that? You might think it's because they cheated their way there and stepped on others to get what they wanted. Maybe they did, maybe they didn't. What I can tell you is that the Laws of the Universe do not play favorites. The only rule is that if you use them, they work, and if you don't use them, they don't work. I bet you could look at your life right now and show me several things you planted that you got a harvest from—they just might not be the things you really wanted.

There are a lot of people who are much better at manifesting than they give themselves credit for. There are a lot of people who are living on a planet that provides plenty of natural and healthy food but are eating chemicals and food invented in a lab and complaining that they can't get healthy or lose weight. They have planted unhealthy seeds for years and are reaping the harvest of it—just not the harvest they wanted.

There are people who have continued to work in a job that doesn't fulfill them for years and feel like life isn't fair because they are stuck in a cycle. All of this time, there were more fulfilling jobs, but they kept showing up to the same terrible job and expecting different results. They are manifesting unfulfillment and boredom with their own power of sowing and reaping.

The trick to getting to your next level of success is realizing that you are powerful and can manifest huge things. You just have to pivot away from sowing destruction and decide instead to sow something productive.

THE LAW OF SEEKING AND FINDING

The next universal principle actually goes hand in hand with the last. This law says that you will find whatever you seek.

Have you ever gotten a new car, only to find that all of a sudden everyone else has the same car? I'll never forget when I got my first brand new car. It was a Toyota 4Runner. I got the Platinum package because I thought the rims were really nice and I really liked the touches of chrome on the running boards and door handles. I also drove off the lot feeling pretty special. I knew the 4Runner was a pretty popular SUV, but since I'd bought the Platinum package, I figured mine would be different. I'm an Enneagram three with just enough four wing to be confusing (Google the Enneagram personality types and get ready for a world of fun). The three in me wants to fit in and impress everyone. The four in me (my musician nature) feels the need to be different than everyone else. So, I tend to be the most creative person in my normal friend groups and the most basic person in my creative friend groups. I felt like my 4Runner was the perfect blend of a popular car but with its own touch.

I was wrong. The second I drove off the lot, I started to see 4Runners everywhere, and almost every single one of them was black like mine and had the Platinum package. I had bought the most basic car in the world. That's what it felt like, but is that really the truth? Of course not. The number of 4Runners sold each year is less than 140,000, with a population of 313 million in the U.S. Out of 140K, I doubt more than 50 percent are black and Platinum, with probably only 15 to 20 percent at best. That means there might be 28,000 SUVs like mine in the whole country. That means that 0.0089 of 1 percent of people have an SUV just like mine. That's fewer than one out of every 100,000 people, and only one million people live in Tulsa plus all of its suburbs combined.

Why was I seeing so many cars just like mine? The minute you purchase a vehicle, you make yourself more aware of that car's make and model and all of the special features about it. You have just proven the Law of Seeking and Finding. This is why it can be so dangerous to develop negative thoughts about yourself. Like I mentioned in a previous chapter, our limiting beliefs are constantly looking for a story to justify our fears and excuses.

The same way our brain can spot the chrome door handles on a black 4Runner passing us on the highway is the same way it can identify anything else we program it to look for. If you say day in and day out that you are ugly, you will start to notice every single thing about your body and appearance that you don't like. If you say over and over that you just can't be successful because you've never been good at anything, you will start to see every part of your business that you suck at.

The difference between successful people and unsuccessful people is not their potential; it's just their ability to *see* their potential. Unsuccessful people have trained themselves to find all of their weaknesses, even though their strengths have been there all along. Successful people have trained themselves to find all of their strengths, even though their weaknesses have been there all along.

The person who planted the flower has every right to get that flower. But there are so many people out there actually doing the work it takes to get that flower who are sabotaging the whole process by choosing to see something else. The number one reason people give up on working toward their flower is that they have trained themselves to find lack and failure, so that's all they see. And you can only take so many failures without getting a win before you are destined to give up.

This is why learning how to coach yourself is so important. You need to know the work that needs to be done, but you also have to work to retrain yourself to actually look for and even *receive* those things you want.

There is a really big difference between *wanting* something and *wishing* for something. What I see most people doing is wishing they could have something but not actually wanting it bad enough to make the shifts that are needed to get it.

Even when we think we are willing to make the shifts, we underestimate how much time it will actually take for our seed to grow and how much internal work it will take to allow it to happen.

I have a few affirmations I use to self-coach and work on aligning myself with my Creator. I call them "trust" affirmations. Some of the affirmations I do, like my "because" affirmations, are geared at getting me to do the right work. But my trust affirmations are geared at training myself to trust the Universe and to be patient in waiting for the things I'm working toward.

As I was writing this book, I went through a little funk in my business. I had just released my new Life Coach Certification program and, in its first month, it did six figures. That was amazing! We had thirty people going through the beta round, and I was so high on energy. Between writing this book and creating the curriculum for these future life coaches, I was feeling all the feels. But the very next month, there was no certification to release (we do them in three-month rounds) and my sales in my first business took a hit because of the amount of energy I had put into launching this new program.

It happened again—the same thing I talked about in the intro of my book. I allowed myself to turn a four out of ten problem into a forty out of ten problem. I started thinking, *Maybe this was the wrong move. Maybe launching a new program killed all my other programs. Maybe now that I'm certifying life coaches, no one else thinks my other groups apply to them anymore.*

I got in a mental funk. I put out a mini course that usually gets everyone super-excited. Usually, my mini courses get 200 to 300 signups, make several thousand dollars for very little work, and I have a super-high upsell rate into my other courses. Before it's all said and done, the mini course sales add to the upsell and so bring in tens of thousands of dollars over a one-week span. This one got seventy to eighty signups, and only ten to fifteen people were even showing up for the calls. Almost no upsells.

What is going on? I thought to myself. For a few weeks, I was talking myself off the figurative ledge day after day. I would crank up my motivation playlist on Spotify and push through my workouts. I was showing up on calls with even more pre-workout in my system, but people were just not responding.

It turns out that one of the companies I work with a lot was having a *huge* slump in their whole company. A company full of health and fitness coaches (probably half of the company has done one of my training sessions at some point) had the biggest slump in recent history. As the world was opening back up after a long pandemic, more people than ever were heading back to the gym and wanted nothing to do with virtual programs. They wanted to take a class with their friends that they had missed out on for the last year and a half. They wanted to get out of the house and see real people in person.

I'm usually really good about not responding to anyone else's energy. But it got me. Their lack of sales was causing fewer people to sign up for my courses, and my confidence was taking a hit. The ones who were in my courses were losing hope and avoiding the calls altogether.

Thankfully, I finally pulled my head out of my ass. I asked myself some powerful questions: *When did you get so spoiled that you need other people to be excited? Remember your whole first year when no one in the world but your mom and sister liked your posts, but you did it anyway? Remember when you met every person you knew at Starbucks to give them free coaching and not one single person ended up hiring you? Remember when only eight people showed up at your first event and you gave the most powerful presentation to this day?*

I asked myself, *Why were you so excited: because people were cheering for you or because you knew people needed you? What daily tasks were you doing that lit you up and filled your tank?*

I realized that in raising a sales team this year, which was absolutely amazing, I had grown lazy with some of the things on my daily to-do list that had kept my confidence growing. Another random thing: I had started listening to a lot of audiobooks and had gotten away from sitting down with a physical copy of a book and a highlighter. It's great to listen on the go for extra learning time, but there's something magical and intentional about sitting down and reading a book, with no other distractions.

I got back to sowing the right seed by *CRUSHING* my to-do list. It felt amazing. But I also knew I needed to step up my trust game. I needed to spend some extra time meditating on trust affirmations.

After I crushed my to-do list, I went out to the pool. I put on some relaxing music, got in my pool hammock (the best pool floatie in the world), and allowed myself to just float around. I pulled out one of my oldest trust affirmations in the book and said over and over and over, "I'm in the right place, at the right time, connecting with the right people, and learning the next right lesson."

I did this for fifteen to thirty minutes, just depending on how long I had until the kids got home from school. I woke up the next day feeling like a champion. I crushed my to-do list, made time for reading a physical copy of a book, and headed out to the pool to do my affirmations.

"I'm in the right place, at the right time, connecting with the right people, and learning the next right lesson."

Fast-forward a few days, and I got a text from someone who had been number one in that same health and fitness company. It read, "Josh, I need help. Some of the things I was doing aren't working anymore and I think I need a PUSH Coach. I also have three other friends who need your help, too."

That conversation led to a few more conversations and led to setting up a workshop in Scottsdale to meet with another five people.

Those conversations led to putting on a Virtual Leadership Summit for both their company and for anyone else who wanted to attend.

Total coincidence or not, a new friend I had just met via a podcast lives in Scottsdale, and we decided to meet up while I was there.

Another coincidence: one of my mentors put together a last-minute engagement party and invited Jenny and me to attend, where we would get to spend the day with an entire group full of other successful entrepreneurs. This event was taking place in the same city that one of my best friends, Robb Pearson, lived in. I got to spend one day with Robb and another day at the engagement party.

All of this because I flipped a switch. You could say that I raised my frequency. The reality is, all of the people I connected with within one to two weeks were all people I'd already had connections with in one way or another. They were like the Platinum 4Runners that had always been on the street. But now I was looking for them.

The reality is, I could have flipped that switch at any time. But I got busy creating resources for my Life Coach Certification program and forgot that the *best version of me* can figure anything out.

I got caught up in the low energy of a few of my clients and forgot that the *best version of me* will always figure it out.

Maybe I got too dependent on my sales team and marketing and forgot that the *best version of me* will figure it out.

As I'm writing this book, I'm still human. I still forget sometimes just how powerful I really am when I feed my heart and starve my doubts. That's why we all have to keep coaching ourselves. No matter how far you think you've come, no matter how far ahead you may get, you have to keep putting work into the best version of yourself.

I've said so many times, the best version of you or the worst version of you is only three to six months away. The one you become has everything to do with the choices you make each day.

You can reap anything you sow. But remember, you will also have to put intentional effort into *seeking* it. You can't just work for it; you also have to imagine it, believe you can have it, and call out to it! That is how you get the Universe on your side: you understand that the Universe is *already* on your side. The Universe has given you all you need. All of the black 4Runners, health, wealth, and so on are sitting right under your nose. You just have to seek if you want to find.

I bargained with life for a penny,
And life would pay no more.
However, I begged at evening
When I counted my scanty store.
For life is just an employer,
He gives you what you ask,
But once you set the wages,
Why, you must bear the task.
I worked for a menial's hire,
Only to learn, dismayed,
That one wage I had asked of life,
Life would have willingly paid.

—Excerpt from *Think and Grow Rich*
by Napoleon Hill

COACHING QUESTIONS

1. What are three things you need to do daily to work toward your goals?

_____

_____

_____

2. What are a few ways you can make sure you are working on the underground process of growth and not just obsessing over the external growth of your flower (dream)?

_____

_____

_____

3. How many times have you noticed the make and model of your car on the road?

_____

_____

_____

4. What are you willing to do to find your dreams as easily as you find your car?

_____

_____

_____

6

PUKE GOALS

In December 2016, I was reflecting on my first couple of years of working with clients. I was using some coaching questions to try to dissect why some of my clients were having such incredible results while others had little to no results. Just to be clear, coaching yourself is all about reflecting for the sake of learning, not for the sake of judging. I wasn't asking, *Why did I fail so many people?* As you have already learned, anything that brings judgment or shame is not from your heart and cannot help you find the best version of you or any productive answers.

Instead, I was asking, *Is there something I could learn that would help more people?*

Thinking through the people who had the biggest results, I was trying to determine if there was anything specific they all had in common. Did they have a common skill? Did I meet them in a similar social circle? What could I find that would help me to determine why they had more success?

And then it came to me. When you ask enough growth questions, you'll find that somehow answers just show up. Growth questions force you to bypass your head and go straight to your heart, where the answers live. I realized that all of my greatest success stories came from people who came to me and said things like "Josh, I have this crazy goal. I don't even know if it's possible. In fact, others have said it's not realistic. But I really want to do it."

Each time, this person would be almost in tears. These weren't tears of fear, pressure, or sadness; they were tears of excitement. When I got remarried in 2021, I must have cried five hundred times on my wedding day. Having gone through a rough divorce years before, finding my soul mate and someone who made me better in every single way was just so much joy and excitement I couldn't handle it. And even though there were fears with stepping into a new season of life, they were fears accompanied by an exhilarating feeling of excitement for what could be.

Those were the kinds of tears these clients were crying. Tears knowing there was something at risk, but they wanted to do it anyway.

Each time, I would look them in the eyes and say, "It does sound crazy. But you came to the right person because that's what I help people do."

A huge smile of relief would come over their faces as they realized that someone believed in them and felt confident about helping them get what they really wanted.

I realized that the people who had the most success working with me were people who came with *urgency*. Urgency is one of the biggest hacks to performance in any area of your life. To be clear, I want you to understand what urgency is *not*, so you don't take this chapter wrong.

Urgency is not putting negative pressure on yourself to do something that others want you to do. It is not putting guilt or shame on yourself to try to force yourself to perform out of fear. Urgency is simply finding out what you really, *really* want and then giving yourself a deadline that scares you just enough to get you to actually take action. There is a really big difference between urgency and rushing. Urgency is the demand you put on yourself to show up, whereas rushing is usually the demand you put on others or the Universe to try to make it happen for you.

I realized that urgency was the game-changer for my clients but had also been the game-changer for me. Rewind back to the beginning of 2015—I had just ended my first year as a life coach, making only $500 and two sales.

I knew I needed to create a new intensity, or this was going to take me fifty years to build. I sat down with a large calendar and did something crazy. I wrote a big number ten at the top of the month. I was going to try to sign ten new clients in one month. This was five times the number of clients I had signed the whole year before. But I knew I needed a challenge.

Then I went down each week and wrote a three at the end of each week. I didn't want to put a two and set myself up to go below my goal, so the only thing I could do was write a three and go over my goal. I sat there looking at my calendar, realizing I needed to have more results this week than I had the previous year. And I felt it. I felt this thing that I now call urgency. I knew that it was time to get serious and make some huge adjustments to how I was approaching my business.

I sat down and coached myself with some questions. I realized I was spread in too many directions, trying to drive all over Tulsa to meet up with potential clients. I was also listening to too many podcasts that were giving business hacks that made me think I needed a website, a podcast, YouTube videos, and everything else in the world. I was getting too distracted to do anything well. Something that J Max had taught me was that nothing in your life changes until you change something you do daily. So, if you're not doing it daily, it's not changing anything. And if you're doing too many things, there's no way you can do them daily.

I asked myself, *What could I do daily that would build up consistent momentum for my business and help me reach these new goals?* I realized that it could be a lot easier than I was making it. What I really needed to do was make sure I stuck to my personal growth plan so that I didn't lose my confidence (I would do affirmations on the way to work, listen to an audiobook on the way home, and read ten pages of a book before bed). I needed to post on social media every day to let people know I was here and doing positive things. I needed to add new friends every day on Facebook so that more people would see my positive posts. Last, and most critical, I needed to message people on Facebook and Instagram every single day to offer them a free call.

I don't actually remember if I hit my goal the first month, but I do remember that I started hitting my goal after two or three months of this level of focused action. By the summer of 2015, I had grown to thirty clients and, even charging less than any other coach in the world, I now had the confidence and network to start making even bigger moves. By the end of the year, my one-on-one time was completely booked, and I had to start launching group coaching courses to teach more people in less time. I ended that year by walking away from my day job and having my first two five-figure months.

Back to the end of 2016, I realized that urgency was the key ingredient for both my most successful clients and myself. So, I put together an email for all of my one-on-one clients that told them in the nicest way possible that I was looking to work with people in 2017 who had very specific goals. I was looking for people who had big and scary goals and were willing to put in extra focus and intensity to reach them. I told them that if they weren't looking to reach crazy goals, working with me would no longer be a good fit. I lost half of my clients with that email, and it was the best thing that could have happened.

I would no longer have to endure hour-long conversations with people who had no intentions of doing anything with them. I would no longer have to pretend to be excited about someone just becoming a little better or leaning on me for motivation. I could now do what I was really born to do: *PUSH* others to reach their full potential.

I started telling people on my monthly webinars not to even join my groups unless they had big goals and were willing to do the work it would take. I even did a Health Bet for Your Business, where people put in extra money toward a pot of cash that they could earn back by doing all of the activities on my business tracker. I started making urgency the core of everything I did and, as a result, my clients started seeing more results. My testimonials started to blow up with people who were reaching goals they had only dreamed of.

I even changed my official title from life coach to PUSH Coach—something I made up to communicate the kind of energy I wanted people to expect from me. I changed my social media from Legacy Leadership to Josh Coats PUSH Coach. I was no longer going to be the friend you could call to make you feel better; I was going to be the coach you hired to get results!

The more I preached on having these larger-than-life goals that demanded more action and ownership, the more I heard people say things like "Ok, I just wrote down the goal I've always wanted and now I feel like puking." I heard those words on call after call in both one-on-one calls and group calls. This led me to eventually say, "Ok, well, let's puke together."

#letspuketogether is still the main hashtag I have my clients use on large webinars to participate in giveaways and challenges. And with time, I've gone on to call these crazy goals Puke Goals.

I want to teach you why urgency is so important and how quickly it can change your whole life without making any other drastic changes.

URGENCY CREATES FOCUS

One of the number one reasons people struggle to reach their next level of success in life is simply a lack of focus. I've worked with six- and seven-figure earners who have got so far on work ethic and then find themselves stuck. They can't figure out why they've plateaued and can't seem to figure out how to move forward. Usually, they are people who, at one point or another, had something to fight for that forced them to have a strict to-do list and be productive. But when the bills are no longer a challenge and they don't have something to fight for, their days become less focused, their to-do lists become less urgent, and they tend to coast on the momentum of yesterday.

Others who are just starting out on their goals get caught up in perfectionism, fear, or self-doubt. As a result, most online entrepreneurs spend more time designing logos and graphics than talking to potential clients.

I've had many moments on my health journey where I had a specific goal or event that I wanted to look good for, so I was incredibly focused on my nutrition and workouts for three to six months. But when the goal is reached or the event is over, it's so easy to go back to just eating healthy-ish and working out every day, but without the same focus and intensity.

The second you set a big goal, you will realize that something inside you shifts. You realize that you no longer have time for the same BS you used to do with your time. You realize that if this is going to happen, you have to be more focused than ever before. You have to create to-do lists, you have to track and measure progress, and you have to show up.

Most people are scared to death of setting big goals because they assume they are too busy to be more productive. The thought of trying to achieve more makes them think that I want them to stay at the office all night or work out four hours a day. The funny thing is that urgency actually does the opposite. It forces you to get more done in less time. It takes someone from taking selfies at the gym to showing up early so that they don't have to share space with anyone else. It takes someone from overthinking logos and colors to messaging more people who could pay them. It takes them from needing everything to be perfectly figured out to just going for it and committing to learn on the go.

URGENCY BREEDS CREATIVITY

When I quit my day job at the end of 2015, I had a fresh sense of excitement for the year ahead. I had found a way to make $48K in my second year of business doing it part-time. What could I accomplish with a year of working full-time in my business? I was reading a book by Grant Cardone called *The 10X Rule* (still one of my favorites), and he encourages you to add a zero to the end of your goal. The idea is that everyone underestimates how much energy and effort it takes to reach a goal. So, if you want to make $100K, you should just go ahead and aim for $1 million, and that way, even if you come up short, you'll still crush your original goal of $100K.

So, I decided to take the amount of money I made detailing cars, about $40K, and try to 10X that with my first full year of working full-time for myself. Someone who had grown up never having enough money to travel, thought eating at Applebee's was "fancy," and had almost been evicted multiple times as an adult was going to try to make $400K in one year!

I had already fixed my focus the year before by coming up with a daily to-do list. But now I would need more. I couldn't do enough free calls to sign clients to make $400K and live to tell about it. That would just be too many calls with too many people. Plus, I didn't have time to work with that many clients anyway. This is when I was still only charging about $100 a call. I would have had to do 4,000 calls, or about eleven one-hour sessions a day, seven days a week, to make that much money.

I knew I needed to find a creative way to make more money in less time. I had already launched some group coaching programs, so I felt that was the best thing, to put my focus and energy there. But at around $200 a person, that was still 2,000 people I needed to sell a course to, and I decided I wasn't willing to message that many people on Facebook. There had to be a better way.

I was at an event where someone was speaking on the power of Periscope, a social media platform that was replaced by Facebook Live. While she was selling the entire audience on using this new platform, she mentioned something that changed my life. It's funny because she wasn't even trying to sell anything about Facebook Ads, but somewhere in her speech, she mentioned how she had used Facebook Ads for years and that it was her biggest ROI of any other form of investing she did in her business.

I was sitting there in a trance as she went on to talk more and more about a platform that everyone else in the room bought into, a platform that completely flopped several months later, and I was hearing a different message. When she mentioned Facebook Ads, something deep inside me shot up and said, "That's it!"

I had already seen her ads popping up in my own feed, day after day. Between her and Lewis Howes, the right column of my feed was filled with their ads every single day. Their ads were showing up so often that I had even set a secondary goal in my business to take over the news feed as much as she had taken over my feed.

Everyone else went home and poured hours into Periscope. Many of them bought her course on how to monetize Periscope. But I went home and started researching Facebook Ads. I was mentioning this whole process to a client who mentioned she had an ads course that she had never used. I offered to give her the next session for free if she allowed me to have her login info. She agreed. I spent the next six months in ads school. For thirty to forty-five minutes every night, I watched videos. I experimented with things I was taught. I would sometimes pause videos to write an ad, only to learn five minutes later something I had just done was wrong and I would have to go back and make edits. But I just kept doing everything I was told. I kept tweaking and experimenting like a mad scientist.

A few months later, an ad for one of my courses went viral. It started to get ten to fifteen messages a day from people who were interested. In fact, it worked so well, I almost turned off the ad because I couldn't keep up with everyone who was interested in purchasing. Thankfully, I had a lifesaving moment where I decided it would make more sense to hire someone to manage the comments and questions than to turn off an ad that was making me money left and right.

Over time, ads became my new thing. In 2015, I became the master of turning a Facebook conversation into a free call and then using that call to convert people into one-on-one clients. In 2016, I became the master of using ads to get people into my inbox and eventually used ads to get people into large webinars, where I taught free value and then pitched at the end of the call. I had nights where I made up to $20K from a one-hour sales call.

Fast-forward to December 31, 2016, and I hit my $400K mark in revenue around 9 pm, within a few minutes of a message I got from one of my one-on-one clients letting me know she had hit her goal, too!

Setting a big goal is scary, but it forces you to dig into a deeper part of yourself to find answers that your brain doesn't have. It is one of the ways to bypass your head voice and to force your heart voice to speak up.

When you go after something bigger than you've ever gone after before, you will find that you have things living on the inside of you that are just waiting to be birthed! You have more creativity than you realize. I say this affirmation every day, and I hope it will also inspire you: "I am a creator. I have my Creator's ideas and energy flowing through my veins."

URGENCY DEMANDS OWNERSHIP

Pretend for a minute that you have left the house for the night and your kids (or pets) are home with a babysitter. You've been out all night having drinks and enjoying yourself (or maybe just at Target trying everything on!). On your way home, you realize there's smoke coming from your neighborhood. Strange. You get to your neighborhood and realize that the smoke is coming from your street. As you round the corner onto your street, it is clear that smoke is coming from your house! Your house is up in flames. So, you race your car up the street. You have no idea whether or not your loved ones are ok. You drive up into the front yard, not even caring that you just demolished your lawn and shrubs and run to the door.

Somewhere in between the car and the house, you lose your keys. You're in such a frantic state that you have no idea what happened. Maybe they fell out in the car, maybe they're buried in the bottom of your purse. All you know is that the front door is locked, your loved ones are probably inside, and you have no keys. What do you do? Do you kick down the door? Punch through a window? Run through the wall? Yes, yes, and hell, yes! You *find* a way to get in because you have no other choice!

Now, lost keys ... Let's take away the fire and take away your loved ones being home. Do you still kick down the door and ruin your new shoes? Or do you go sit in your car, call a locksmith, and play on your phone until someone shows up to get you in? My guess is the latter.

Here's the thing. I've spent hundreds, if not thousands, of hours on calls with entrepreneurs who have a burning desire to reach their full potential and help others do the same. I've listened to story after story on one-on-one calls, in my training groups, and at team retreats I've done around the country. I've heard people tell me how desperate they are for something to change in their lives. I've heard stories of people with jobs that are eating their souls and keeping them away from making memories with their kids. Stories of stay-at-home parents who want nothing more than to relieve the financial pressures on a spouse who is overworked and underpaid. Stories of people buried in debt so deep, they have no hope of ever having any type of financial freedom. People who want to travel, send their kids to the best schools, give to charity, and raise funds for others in need.

From what I've seen, there are a whole lot of houses on fire, and a lot of people sitting around in their cars, playing on their phones, waiting for a locksmith to come save the day. But "I don't have a big enough following," "I don't know how to talk to people," or "Why would anyone want to sign up with me?" just sounds to me like "I don't care enough about my family/ health/future/purpose to run into the burning building."

The truth is, you have the same resources as everyone else. You're just looking for something easier. One of my best-selling trainings that I ran for several years for online entrepreneurs was full of so much content, you couldn't possibly walk away and *not* know how to sell. People tell me all the time how much they loved the training and how inspiring and impactful it was. In reality, only 10 to 15 percent of the people who took the training actually did anything with it.

How do I know? Because the views on the week-four videos were less than half of the views on week one. Because by week three, hardly anyone was even checking into the Facebook group we provided. And because the people who did the work, that 10 to 15 percent, ended up having crazy positive testimonials. One sales rep went top 10 in her whole company from what she learned from this $199 training.

So, I decided to change the game. In 2018, I launched a training called the PUSH Mastermind (now called Heart + Hustle + Harmony). In this group, I gave people the same daily activities list, but instead of giving them twenty videos to view, we just had a once-a-week teaching call. Instead of trying to teach people *how* to build their businesses, I put the focus on just *doing* the work.

It had daily challenges, weekly call-outs for falling behind on activities, and weekly recognition for people who got results. Instead of hearing things like "O Gaaaaaawd, you dropped so many truth bombs, Josh!" (I'm saying this in my best diva voice), I started hearing things like "I've never worked this hard at any time in my entire business, and it feels *good* to be this productive!" Instead of having 10 to 15 percent of the enrollees stick it out, we had over 90 percent. The testimonials started piling up!

I get that my "house on fire" analogy is a little extreme, but that's how serious I am about helping people create their best lives. I'm continually reminding my PUSH groups that the demons you don't face are the ones you automatically pass on to your kids. You can tell your kids all day and night to chase their dreams. But if you don't *show* them what that looks like, will they? I can promise you that they'll duplicate what you *do*, not what you *say*.

Do you really want to tell your kids that they're not "outgoing enough," "pretty enough," or "skilled enough" to make their dreams come true? Do you want to teach them to live from their head instead of their heart?

The reality is that your kids are going to come to you at some point and ask you for advice. Maybe they want to make the team, maybe they want to go to a certain college. Whatever it is, they will come to you when they struggle. They will say things from their head voice like "Mom/Dad, I don't think I'm good enough. I don't think I'm smart enough. I don't think I'm pretty enough."

In that moment, you will obviously tell them that you believe in them. You will tell them that they can do anything they put their mind to. But will they really believe the person who hasn't lived that example first?

At some point, we have to ask ourselves if our advice is full of shit or if our excuses are full of shit. We either really believe that anyone can accomplish their dreams and we need to stop making excuses, or we need to believe that no one can and stop giving advice. But if everyone can, that includes you, too!

Ownership isn't just about you. It's also about what you're willing to do for your family and for the world around you. Even if your house isn't on fire. Even if you have plenty of money in the bank, a boat, and a white picket fence. Do you have enough to fund your favorite charity? Do you have enough to build orphanages in Africa? Do you have enough to end world hunger? Then you're not done yet.

Grant Cardone says, "Success is your moral and ethical obligation." And I believe in that statement so much. If your house isn't on fire, I believe very strongly that *your mission* should be to help as many other people as possible put their fires out. As long as you are breathing, there is work to do— because there are others who need you! Living anything less than your *full* potential is a slap in the face to both your Creator and the rest of creation!

If you take the time to set your own Puke Goals, you'll find a whole new level of potential is just waiting for you. This is one of the keys to coaching yourself and others to the next level of success. In fact, it's one of the reasons I do something called a Breakdown Session with my one-on-one clients. It's a process of asking questions that force you to dig in and find what you *really* want in life and to create a plan and process for how to make it happen.

One of the things I'm always emphasizing to the life coaches in my program is how to set their own Puke Goals to make sure they are also tapping into their own heart voices and creating something significant in their own lives as they coach others to do the same. They go through their own Breakdown Session, so they'll be equipped to put others through the same process.

I wanted to give you a few of the questions that I use for the Breakdown Session to help you get started on your first Puke Goal. Feel free to use these questions to help others you are leading and coaching.

COACHING QUESTIONS

1. Imagine yourself one year out. Now imagine that I could remove all of the obstacles, all of the pain, all of the time, and all of the energy it would take to get what you really want. What would you reach out and take? What would you want in your life if it didn't cost you anything and you could just have it handed to you?

_____

_____

_____

_____

_____

2. Imagine we are at a retreat together one year from now. I walk up to you and say, "I am so proud of you for reaching that goal! That was *amazing*! Would you mind sharing with my clients the top three things you did to make that goal happen?" What would your three things be?

_____

_____

_____

3. What can you do on a daily basis to put yourself on track to do the three things you mentioned in number two? (We can't know for sure, but we can use our heart voice to help us make accurate predictions.)

_____

_____

_____

4. What is your head voice trying to tell you about this goal and your ability to reach it? What are the thoughts of doubt, fear, and weakness that are going to try to hold you back?

_____

_____

_____

5. What does the voice of love, hope, excitement, purpose, passion, and faith have to say about your ability to reach your goal?

_____

_____

_____

6. How can you remind yourself daily of the heart voice from number five and begin to reprogram yourself to believe in your ability to reach this goal?

_____

_____

_____

7. Who will you be accountable to? Who will you share this process with whom you can trust to believe in and encourage you but also call you out when you try to run away?

_____

_____

_____

7

ENTREPRENEURSHIP— HEART + HUSTLE + HARMONY

I couldn't write an entire book without talking about the thing I am most passionate about. I mentioned how falling in love with life coaching caused me to pursue a business coaching others. I don't want to assume that everyone in the world is called to entrepreneurship, but I do believe that there is a piece of it living inside all of us. Entrepreneurship is simply the desire to give your flavor to the world through some type of creative process. Sometimes this looks like having an online business, other times it means starting a nonprofit, or it may even be leading some type of social reform.

Regardless of how this looks for you, I wanted to write a nontraditional chapter on this subject. I have tons of materials on my website on how to market, sell, and use social media. So, I wanted to keep this chapter in alignment with the concept of this book and look at something that is a little more growth-oriented.

In 2020 the world was hit by a global pandemic. I'll never forget sitting on my couch watching a basketball game when the announcement came across the bottom of the screen: NBA season canceled. And within a few days, every major sports league, professional and college, had also canceled their seasons.

My business was doing amazing and, although I was a little concerned about what a pandemic might do to my sales, I ended up running into a problem I could have never predicted.

The shift in the world led to a lot of people being out of jobs, which actually made online businesses like mine skyrocket. But I found myself sitting around the house in the evenings feeling lonely. My kids go to their mom's half of the time, so they kept me busy on days they were with me, but on days they were gone, I sat alone in an empty house scrolling through thousands of shows and movies available and just feeling empty. Jenny worked most evenings, so she would be in her office. She is a virtual therapist and during that season was working with clients who were only available in the evenings.

What was wrong with me? I had always been such a happy and motivated person. I was still motivated during the day when there was work to do, but I just felt lethargic and blah all evening.

Thankfully, I'm a trained life coach, so I took some time to coach myself as I'm teaching you to do in this book. I started asking myself questions. *Why do I feel this way? What is different now than before? What are the times I feel like this?*

The more I thought of it, the more I realized that, before the world shut down, I would spend my afternoons working in coffee shops, where there was at least noise around, people to meet, and baristas who sometimes knew me by name. Just getting away for a few hours in the afternoon would rejuvenate me. On evenings that my kids were gone, I would sometimes stay late at the coffee shop and hang out. Other nights, I would go to a local restaurant or grab a drink at one of my favorite cocktail bars.

I started to wonder, *Am I really a happy person, or have I just always found ways to stay busy?*

This question hit me hard! I realized that there is a really big difference between being happy and being motivated. I was motivated, which led me to do a lot of things most people wouldn't do. Like growing a business or showing up at a random cocktail bar and meeting the bartender so I would have someone to talk to. But that doesn't make me happy; it just makes me feel good.

I realized that my whole life, I had always found a way to be busy so I didn't have to be alone. I happened to be in training with one of my mentors, Gerard Adams, who was making us do something he called the H5. There were five different Hs he wanted us to focus on that were all around having full and harmonious lives. From that training, I pulled out my favorite three and started making it part of all my online training.

I created a formula that I call Heart + Hustle + Harmony. These were new words for something I had technically always done, but this global pandemic was forcing me to dig in and find new and even healthier ways to do it.

HEART

You have already learned how the heart is the real you. This is your divine nature and your constant connection to your Creator. I started doing very specific morning routines to make sure that my heart was connected to my day and my work. I was already doing a few good things, but I saw this as a great time to reflect and make this routine even better.

I start out every day by taking half a scoop of pre-workout, setting a five-minute timer, and acknowledging my Creator. I go through all of the expressions of the heart and say things like "I am acknowledging the voice of Hope today. I am acknowledging the voice of Love today. I am acknowledging the voice of Purpose today." I start off with words from the graphic I shared in the Head vs. Heart chapter and just see where it goes. These words usually inspire other new heart words that are powerful to me.

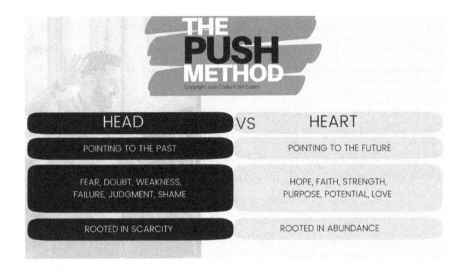

Then I write down all of my goals, schedule out my day, and write down three things I am grateful for. Finally, I say my list of affirmations. Once I have done all of these things, I take the rest of my pre-workout and jump into my workout. It might sound silly to say that my workout is part of my heart routine, but for me it is. I turn on motivational tracks on Spotify and push myself during this time to tap into my inner strength and potential.

Here's why it's so important to start your day off with the heart routine, no matter what you do for a living. If your heart is where your purpose and strength live, this sets you up to live each day from your inner power. Whatever it is you need to accomplish in life, I can promise that you will need this power.

I see entrepreneurs all the time investing thousands of dollars in training that promises the perfect formula for converting more sales. One person says it's your ad copy, another says it's your landing page, another says it's your social media content, and on and on and on. Isn't it funny how there can be just "one thing" that everyone needs and yet all of the "gurus" seem to disagree on what that one thing is?

The reality is, people who are too good at sales sometimes take advantage of your weaknesses and insecurities. Just like in the diet world, people know you want results now, so they twist the truth to tell you what you want to hear so they can get your money.

I'm so sick of this bullshit that I'm personally working very hard to rebrand my whole online culture around speaking to the heart instead of tricking people through their doubts and fears.

This goes deeper than just business. As a parent, I have so many doubts and insecurities. I'm doing my best every day, but every time one kid lashes out, I'm worried that somehow it's my fault. Maybe I should be more strict, like my parents. Maybe I should be less strict, like some other parents I know.

When you are in that place of doubt and fear, just about anyone can convince you of the "right" way to do something. Starting off your day in your heart is about finding your clarity, your certainty, your strength, and your *power*.

It's about going to work and going to the world with something you believe in so much that you don't need someone else's solution. You realize that *you* are the solution. You have the magic living on the inside of you, and you don't need to pay a guru to borrow their magic.

My training groups are less about "fixing" people's business problems and more about teaching them simple principles and helping them realize their own power.

If you are someone who leads or mentors others, it's that much more important to make sure you are living from your heart. Like having kids, others will often trigger your limiting beliefs and fears. If you aren't careful, you will start thinking that their failures are your fault. We should always be looking for ways to improve our systems and accountability, but sometimes people are just bad clients or employees.

We have to stop taking the results of others so personally. Let me remind you of a powerful principle I shared earlier in this book. You have to stop looking to others for the affirmation and confirmation you should have given yourself when you woke up.

If you are living from your heart, you will show up with the confidence and vision that demand respect. People will want to follow you because they see that you don't need their approval. Like the stereotypical high school quarterback or captain of the cheerleading squad, people tend to follow the people who don't "need" others to follow.

I'm not saying to be an ass. I just mean to raise your frequency to a place where people want to chase you because they can see you are going somewhere. Leaders should not spend their time chasing others; they should step up to such a high level of purpose that others chase them!

HUSTLE

The word "hustle" is being turned into a four-letter word on social media. I have seen so many social media influencers mocking the hustle and choosing to focus more on the Law of Attraction. Here's the thing: the Law of Attraction is *real*. You really do find what you seek. But as I mentioned earlier in this book, you also reap what you sow. You can't separate the two laws.

Here's what I have observed. I have watched entrepreneurs who didn't learn the harmony aspect I'm about to teach you, who worked all day and night for four or five years, made millions of dollars, and then got emotionally burned out. They now get triggered by people who say things like "Stop watching Netflix and work on your side hustle." The reality is, you don't have to stop watching Netflix altogether, but it is a little ridiculous when people who watch five hours of Netflix a day say they don't have time for a side hustle.

Please remember that all personal growth applies to every area of your life or it's not personal growth. I want you to try waking up every morning and imagining yourself skinnier (or more muscular) faster. Then go eat anything you want. Does this person actually get in better shape?

The answer is no. You can imagine being healthier all day and, while that might make you a happier person (which is also important), it won't actually change your physical state unless you do the workout and follow the meal plan.

So, if you can't change your body by just imagining good things, why would you be able to change your business? The hustle is necessary, and it is not evil. But there are a few things you need to know about it if you don't want it to take over your life.

First, always use some type of tracker. I have used trackers on myself since year two, and it's something I put my clients on. A tracker is simply a list of daily items you need to do every day to grow your business. Notice I said to *grow* your business, not *manage* it. Everyone has things they have to do to manage the business, but that does not lead to new customers or more money. Most people spend all day and night answering existing messages and making graphics, but very few people ever take the time to do what is necessary to grow.

So, what are the activities needed to grow? You just need to follow my Expand + Engage + Convert method. This method says that every day, I need to expand to someone who doesn't know me, I need to engage the people who already know me but haven't purchased anything, and I need to ask people who haven't purchased to purchase. I can't just post every day on social media and expect that people will randomly message me and ask where they can pay. Sales is a numbers game, so unless you have 100K followers, you will almost *never* get messages from people who want to give you money. Thankfully, I grew my business to $40K a month before having a large following, and you can, too! If you want more details on the daily tasks you should be doing and ongoing training on sales and marketing, make sure to check out my training for entrepreneurs on my site (www.joshcoats.com).

Second, you need to have a clock-out time. One of the hardest things about being an entrepreneur in this day and age is that our businesses are often available from our phones. This is such a great blessing if you are busy, like I was my first few years in business, but incredibly dangerous if you don't create boundaries. Regardless of what time of the day you work your business, you have to have a time that you are committed to being finished and going to live your life with the people you love!

Third, and this is so important, you need to do some type of trust affirmations when you clock out. This is a way of releasing the hustle energy so that you don't take your work with you, mentally and emotionally. Even if you turn off the phone, if you fail to transition your energy and mentality, you will find yourself thinking all night about what you didn't get done or what you need to do tomorrow. Your family will get the worst of you and, even if you make a million dollars, you won't have anyone to enjoy it with.

I give my clients a full list of trust affirmations. The general idea is that these are things you say to remind yourself that you can only do what you can do and the rest will work out. I believe that I have a 100/100 partnership with my Creator and that when I give 100 percent of what I have, my Creator gives 100 percent too. Having faith in my Creator has given me so much of an advantage over the years. Even when I don't fully believe in myself or my work, I believe that my Creator's touch on my work is more than enough to give it what it needs.

Try saying something like this every day when you clock out: "Because I reap what I sow, I trust that the work I did today is good enough for the harvest I need tomorrow. I can't force or control the future, but I can do my part and trust that my Creator will pick up where I left off."

I try very hard to let go of my work at the end of the day. I personally believe that the more I hold onto it, the less my Creator can do. This is supposed to be a 100/100 relationship, but if I try to take on 150, I only leave 50 for my Creator. And I believe that my Creator does way more with 100 percent than I could ever do with mine!

I also try to remember that my wife and kids need 100 percent too. And if I'm holding onto work, I can't give them my best. To me, that is the greatest hurt, not to fail at business but to feel like I have failed my family. For me, my family was the motivation for building a business. They were my motivation for having all of the conversations in the inbox that felt weird and gross. They were my motivation for reading all of the books and taking all of the courses. Shame on me if I allow all of that work that was supposed to be for them to take over the time I could have given them.

That is why I tell my clients, "Do your shit and get out!" Don't waste a bunch of time doing busywork. Don't play on your phone and call it work. If you're going to have a business, a band, a nonprofit, or even a career, do what is most important to grow it and then clock out. Don't be a wantrepreneur who just likes to have the notebooks, the books, and the hustle T-shirts. Don't be someone who talks about it; be someone who is about it.

HARMONY

My least favorite word in the dictionary is "balance." People tell me all the time that they need to find more balance. They even take a step back from their businesses in the name of balance. What they think they are saying is that this new thing in life is taking over the other areas of their lives, so they need to let it go. What they really need to do is stop letting it take over their lives and understand what harmony is.

I don't know if you know anything about music, but I'm sure you can imagine what a mixer is. It's a large box that all of the microphones and instruments get plugged into at a concert. There is someone who is dedicated to controlling the volume levels and EQ on all of the different inputs to make sure the band sounds good.

Now, in order to "balance" out the sound, I want you to imagine that the sound technician turns the volume of every single instrument and every single singer to the exact same level. Do you know what that would sound like? It would sound like shit. Because the backup singers aren't supposed to be as loud as the lead singer. The bass guitar is often louder than the other guitars for certain genres, and in other genres the guitar might be much louder than the bass guitar. The drums are, of course, always turned up to 10 (that's just a joke because I'm a drummer).

The sound tech's job is to feel out the music and decide what is best for each song and even each part of the song. They are constantly moving the knobs up and down to find the perfect balance. If you understand that kind of balance, I would be totally ok with you using the word. True balance or, as I like to call it, "harmony" is when you understand that all of the different pieces in your life need different levels of attention depending on the season, the month, the week, or even the day.

I have my kids 50 percent of the time, so on those days I check out earlier and do a lot more family activities. Days that I don't have my kids, I schedule my evening calls and date night with my wife. I am able to look at my life and move the knobs around to make the best song I can.

Let's talk about harmony for your business. Because I believe that most people who understand the element of hustle get burned because they don't know how to shift the knobs. Some people don't even have this instrument plugged in.

When it comes to your business, harmony is identifying the things that counteract the energy of the hustle.

I have always said that the quickest way to find the voice of Creator is to think in terms of purpose and potential. Your purpose is your desire to help others, and your potential is your ability to grow your own knowledge and skills. But during the 2020 pandemic, I realized that both of those things promote hustle. I had never found the other side of that. The more I meditated on this, I came up with a few new words that I believe create harmony for purpose and potential.

I believe that I experience the same level of deepness in my heart when I am discovering or creating.

I believe that we were put on this beautiful planet to enjoy it. I live in Oklahoma but travel all over the country to speak at events. One of my favorite things to do is to discover new cities, new cultures, and of course new scenery. When I am discovering something new or something in nature, I feel alive in a way that completely recharges me. During the pandemic, I wasn't able to travel, but I was able to go to the lake with my paddleboards. I was able to go on walks and look at the stars and the big, beautiful moon. I was able to lie in my hammock and look into the clouds.

Because of this discovery, I actually had a pool installed in our backyard with a beautiful waterfall. Now I go outside every day and float around in my pool while I do my trust affirmations. Sometimes I go out to the pool in between calls or just when I need to recharge and float around and meditate on affirmations.

The other thing that I see as harmony in my life is what I create. When I say creating, I don't mean creating things for my business, even though that can be a positive outlet, too. I mean creating something such as music by playing one of my instruments. Maybe for you it's reading books that are not related to your business. Or maybe you love to paint or draw. Whatever it is, I believe that there is an artist on the inside of all of us, and giving that part of your time will actually open up new spaces on your soundboard that make you feel more alive and make your song more complete.

There are many other ways to embrace harmony, but for the sake of this chapter, the main point that I want to get across is that most people either work too much or work and unplug. I think it's totally fine to unplug, but it's just as important to recharge. Unplugging just means that you put your brain in airplane mode. It's turned off and not producing anything. While this is also a necessity in life, I don't think anyone here needs to be told to watch more Netflix. I think what you probably need more is to be told to make time for recharging—in other words, tapping into your creative nature in a way that actually gives you fuel and makes you more equipped for your purpose and potential.

When I watch Netflix, I don't really get more tired, but I also don't get recharged. I can float around in my pool for fifteen minutes and meditate and, when I'm done, I feel like I got a full night's sleep and am ready to do more. To be clear, that doesn't mean I need to hustle more, but it means I'm able to go into my family time with more energy for my family instead of saying, "Leave me alone—I'm tired from work."

If you have a family, I highly recommend that you practice these harmony activities with your family. Take them to see new things, eat at new restaurants, go for a hike, or paint or draw together. You may not have a place in your business for them to hustle with you, but I think it's so important to not only teach your family to recharge but also experience these things together.

During my first year of living by the Heart + Hustle + Harmony formula, I had my first seven-figure year in business, hired more people, helped and trained more people, and became a better person.

I tell my clients every week on our group calls that the goal is not to just make a lot of money. The goal is to be successful in business *and* in life. I hope you will make that your goal, too! I truly believe that living by the Heart + Hustle + Harmony formula is the way to achieve that!

COACHING QUESTIONS

1. What is the danger of chasing after the hustle without first engaging your heart?

2. What are two to three things you would want to do every morning to start your day off in your heart?

_____

_____

_____

3. Why do you think society is starting to see hustle as such a bad thing?

4. What are the two to three things you need to do every single day to get closer to your goal?

_____

_____

_____

5. What is your biggest struggle when it comes to embracing harmony?

6. What are two to three things you need to do each day to recharge and embrace more harmony?

_____

_____

_____

If you are an entrepreneur, or someone looking to start a business, I highly recommend checking out my 626: The Sprint to Six Figures. This is where I pour my heart and soul into other entrepreneurs to help them to build six figure businesses. Everything you've learned in this book about Head vs Heart is the center of everything I teach around social media, sales, marketing, and leadership. Go to https://www.joshcoats.com/workshop to register for my next free workshop to learn all about it!

8

LEADERSHIP MADE SIMPLE

Leadership is one of the most important subjects on the planet, yet it is the least understood. My book *F*** Leadership* was written in response to the complete misunderstanding of what leadership is. I have mentored 40,000-plus entrepreneurs over the last seven years, and most of them were people who were building businesses and teams and saw a great need for leadership.

Why would I have a book called *F*** Leadership*? Because on call after call, I had people constantly tell me that they weren't good enough leaders to help others. They weren't sure if their processes were good enough. They were worried that they didn't understand enough love languages and personality types. They thought they were too introverted to be sufficient in leading others.

After hearing these doubts and limiting beliefs over and over, one day I just said, "FUCK LEADERSHIP!" I wasn't mad at the actual idea of leadership but more at what people were turning it into. I realized that social media had distorted the idea of leadership, and people were confusing leadership with celebrity.

You see, if our limiting beliefs are constantly looking for a story to justify our fears and excuses, we will automatically try to find the thing in the world that gives us an excuse to give up and never even try. If you are someone who is trying to help others, which I hope you are, then you will no doubt have thoughts and feelings of being unworthy of helping them. As a result, you will look for others to justify this idea.

If you are introverted, you'll immediately follow all of the most extroverted people on the planet on social media. If you think you are too plain, you'll follow the loudest and boldest people. If you are worried that it takes a large following to be a good leader, you will go follow people who have millions of followers.

Here's what most people don't do: take the time to coach themselves with questions that matter. And this is what I have done to help others see what leadership is and isn't. One simple question that I've asked clients and groups over and over: What is your definition of a leader? You see, by using the word "definition," I'm forcing people to go past their feelings and speak from their logic. When I'm coaching someone, I pay close attention to whether they say "I feel like" or "I know that." The difference is where the answer is coming from. If they open a statement with how they feel, I know it's coming from their emotional triggers. What do our emotions do? They overexaggerate everything! But if they lead with what they know, I then know they're speaking from their heart and their logic. Both of these are safe spaces to listen to.

So, when I ask, "What is your definition of a leader?" I start to get responses like "Someone who leads by example," "Someone who cares about others," "Someone who wants to make a difference," and "Someone who shows up, even when it's hard."

In other words, most people agree that being a good leader is more about your heart and actions and less about your fame and fortune. You do not need to have it all figured out to help others. The only thing you have to do to help someone else is to be one step ahead of them.

I want to give you a synopsis of the 4 Ms I wrote about in my last book, and, of course, you can grab a copy at www.joshcoats.com or on Amazon if you want to do a deep dive on this specific topic.

The 4 Ms are the guide to becoming an effective leader in any situation in life. Whether you are creating a business with clients, building a team, parenting, or serving in your community, this is the simplest and most organized system you could follow. And that's what true coaching does: it forces you to create simplicity and organization all at once!

Here are the 4 Ms:

Model

Motivate

Mentor

Multiply

MODEL

The goal of leadership is always to multiply ourselves to some capacity into others. If you are selling a product to a client, you want to multiply your passion for this product to them so they will be regular buyers. If you are building a team, you want to multiply your lessons, work ethic, and character into them so they will become productive leaders on your team. If you are parenting, you want to multiply your core values and ideologies into your children. Multiplication isn't about raising your clone, but it is about passing off something of value that will benefit both them and you.

The number one mistake I see up-and-coming leaders making is that they want to preach their message, but they don't want to live their message. Those who are starting health businesses want to preach about health and fitness all day long, but too often excuse themselves from the very habits they are preaching. Sales managers want to tell everyone else to smile and dial and haven't picked up the phone to call a prospect in ten years. Religious and political leaders want to tell everyone else to do their part for the community; meanwhile, they haven't set foot in the community in years.

The number one thing every leader must do is *model* the work they are asking others to do. You can't possibly multiply hard work into others if you are not working hard yourself. Modeling the right attitude, behavior, and performance is the foundation of the house you are building on. If at any point this foundation cracks, the rest of the house is immediately worthless.

If you are having trouble getting others to buy into your vision, make sure you look in the mirror first. Ask yourself if you are truly living out what you preach, and make sure you are stretching for new goals. One of the biggest problems I have seen is leaders who create massive success and then think they have earned the right to sit on the sideline and coach others. While this makes sense in basketball or football, remember that in those sports the coaches are usually too old to be physically capable of performing the same feats as those they are coaching. Also, remember that in modern-day sports, the coaches almost never make as much as the players, and the coaches are seen as expendable. Owners of sports teams are realizing that the most value is in those who can actually go on the court and make a difference in the score. This does not mean sports coaches are not valuable; I just want to point out that sports is a terrible analogy for what leadership should look like in any other industry.

Imagine if I opened up this book by saying, "I used to be really good at coaching myself, but lately I've been really lacking in my own growth because I've been helping so many other people." Would you want to buy my book?

Imagine if I said, "My business is on the decline, but it's ok because I've been busy helping others grow their businesses."

No one wants to follow the person who talks the talk but can't walk the walk.

Please take this as an encouraging word, not as discouragement. I want you to understand that you can be the best leader in the world by continuing to grow yourself. All leadership starts with self-leadership. You don't have to be loud and outgoing, or have a lot of followers on social media, or live in a mansion. People care more about your character than they do your personality. While this is a challenge to your character, I think it should also be a relief to realize that the Law of Ownership applies to leadership.

By controlling what you can control, you are, by most people's definition, a good leader.

Here are the different areas you will need to model as a leader:

1. Your Actions

The first step to being a good leader is simply leading by example. I want you to make it a goal to be a high performer. We'll chat a little more about that in a minute, but please remember that the only thing it really takes to lead others is to be one step ahead. You do not need to be perfect, but you do need to show up.

Whatever you are trying to motivate others to do, make sure that you also have a list of things you are doing on a regular basis. Do not make excuses. Remember that actions speak louder than words.

Too many leaders spend more time on their presentations and content than they do on their to-do list. If you step up your actions, you can speak from experience instead of needing slides or a planned presentation. I'm not saying you shouldn't use slides or plan your presentation, but there is something powerful about someone who is sharing from the experiences they are currently having instead of requoting something they heard someone else say.

I truly believe that, as leaders, we have to stay in the trenches. We have to find a way to keep challenging ourselves with new goals and new things we are working toward. Those challenges might be different than the challenges our followers are facing, but good luck motivating someone else if you aren't currently being challenged in any way.

I work with a lot of people at a lot of different levels. I don't pretend that the person trying to make their first $10K is having the same challenge as me. But the fact that I am pushing for a new goal and stretching beyond my comfort zone means I have a relevant story and a relevant pain to share with them. The fact that I am still facing pain daily is what gives me the right to speak to their pain.

2. *Your Energy*

Whether you have it or you don't, people notice. Your energy is everything. No one wants to follow a leader who isn't excited about the journey ahead. It's ok to be honest about the fact that the journey will be a challenge, but you need to be excited about that challenge.

I love to share this analogy with my clients. Imagine two women going to a fitness class. One of them shows up early, is always in the front row, and pushes herself every single day. When the instructor says to jump, she jumps as high as she can. She pushes herself every single class to go a little harder and do more than she did the day before. The other woman goes to the exact same class every day. She shows up right as the class starts. She misses the warm-up because she's busy trying to get the perfect selfie so all of her friends know she made it. She sits in the back, where the instructor can't see her and call her out. Each move, she chooses to do the modified or beginner version, even though she doesn't have any type of physical injury that makes her incapable of the more challenging moves. The reality is, she doesn't want to be challenged. She doesn't want to give her all.

Now tell me which of the two will get better results? Both of them work out every day. Both of them are technically doing the same workout. One of them was willing to give her all. She was willing to bring a different kind of energy and, as a result, she got everything the class had to offer.

Your energy will be the difference between getting the bare minimum results and getting the maximum results. In my book *F*** Leadership*, I talk about something I call the Law of Energy. The Law of Energy says that when all other things are equal, the person with the higher vibes will always win.

I recently talked to some new clients who are a ten out of ten in leadership. But their vibes were off. The people they were leading had been making a lot of excuses and had stopped showing up during a trying time in their company.

I explained to them that it didn't matter if they were ten out of ten leaders. If their vibes were four out of ten, there's no way in the world they would attract other powerful leaders. I've heard it said that you attract who you are, not who you want. I'll take that a step further and say that it doesn't matter who you are if you aren't communicating that to the world around you with your energy.

When you have the right energy, it can make up for your lack of a lot of other things. When you don't have the right energy, it doesn't really matter how many other things you have.

3. Your Performance

If you want to lead others, you really need to take your performance seriously. I see way too many people wanting to teach things they have no proof of. I see people who have almost no following and very little engagement on their social media becoming social media coaches. They have some good ideas for what people should do with social media, but they don't want to take the time to grow their own social media. They decided to start charging for ideas they really had no proof of.

People often ask me, "So, as a business coach, did you ever have your own business before you started coaching others?"

I completely understand where they're coming from. They are usually business owners who have had their own level of success. They are wondering if I actually grew my own business before I started offering my advice or if I'm one of those fakers who gives advice about something I've never done before.

I always have to explain to them that I grew my business as a life coach first. I never gave a single piece of business advice until I grew my own business enough to know what the hell I was talking about. As a life coach, my only job was to ask questions and help others become more intentional with what they already knew. I didn't claim to be a "business coach" until I made at least $10,000 in one month. At that point, I stopped and said, *You know, I think I have learned some valuable ways to grow a business that I could actually teach others.*

Your performance will always be one of your greatest assets. Again, I want to remind you that you don't have to be the greatest achiever on the planet, but you do need to be a step ahead of the people you want to lead.

I use this as a constant motivation to grow more and more. I ask myself who I need to become to lead the people I want to lead.

I get the most out of leading people who are six- and seven-figure earners. In order to do that, I have to continuously elevate my own game. I have to always have a new book I'm reading or a new lesson I'm learning. I have to be willing to always push past the limits in my own business.

I don't want you to start seeing your performance through the eyes of guilt and shame. Remember, that does not serve you. Please see this as a challenge to your purpose and potential to become better with each day. See this as a challenge to fully embrace becoming the very best version of yourself!

MOTIVATE

Motivation is the most fun part of leadership that everyone thinks of when it comes to leadership. The word "motivate" is sexy and, if it were a job title, we would probably imagine some beautiful person with all of the energy in the world standing up on stage and inspiring everyone. It's the reason so many companies use bikini models for their commercials.

I will admit that, being an outgoing person myself and someone who is very high energy, for the longest time I thought I was a naturally gifted motivator. When I went through life coach training, the program was to become a public speaker and life coach. I thought that I would go all in on public speaking and maybe learn a little of the life coaching in case I ever needed it. I was wrong.

Life coaching taught me more about being a motivational speaker than anything else I've ever learned. I realized that my version of motivation was very selfish. I thought leaders had the answers, the solutions, and the best ideas, and their job was to deliver those ideas and answers with the most amount of energy possible so that others would join the cause and go along. I was wrong.

Life coaching put me in a position where I was asking questions to others about what they really wanted, what they felt was holding them back, and what they believed needed to be done about it. I learned that people are mostly motivated by the words and ideas that come out of their own heads and hearts.

I then took the data from my one-on-one coaching calls and started turning it into presentations and online courses. Instead of just getting up and speaking from my own thoughts and ideas, I started using the data I had collected on my one-on-one calls. I called this global listening. I took the stories I heard in conversations over and over and used them as a motivational tool for the masses.

For example, if twenty people told me they struggled with motivation and then further coaching uncovered a fear of what others would think of them, I would put together a presentation called How to Get Over the Fear of What Others Think.

As I gave the presentation, people would start to type into the online chat, "OMG, it's like you are in my head!"

The greatest compliment you can ever receive from someone is for them to tell you that you are in their head. This means that you have made a direct connection with their internal thoughts and beliefs. As I've already taught you, you can't change your behaviors or anyone else's without understanding their internal thoughts and beliefs.

Most people try to motivate others by stirring up feelings of excitement and joy. But what happens when they wake up the next day and their old thoughts and beliefs are still there? I have watched leader after leader try to "motivate" others by giving challenge after challenge, teaching after teaching, without addressing the most important issue: their beliefs. I think it's also incredibly important to put together challenges. I love to give tons of incentives and do anything I can do to create positive feelings for my clients. But the positive feelings are not the long-term solution. The positive feelings are just temporary solutions that we should be using to get people to embrace the long-term process of changing their beliefs and behaviors.

With that said, I would love to share a few of the things you can do in this process to help shift these beliefs and behaviors. But if you want to become a master motivator, I highly suggest looking into my life coaching program, where you can get a deep dive on how the belief system works and how you can help others truly transform!

What gets celebrated gets repeated. If you have specific things you want people to do more of, you need to celebrate them more often! Want people to buy more from you? Come up with a way to celebrate them for shopping with you. Want team members to sell more? Celebrate them for their sales. Want kids to clean up more often? Give more high fives and maybe even some ice cream to celebrate them for it.

This is one of the most basic motivational tools that we often forget about. When I was a kid, my parents told me that they would pay me $1 for every goal I scored on the soccer team. When I was four or five, I was pretty shy and laid-back. Soccer was fun, but I didn't really want to be aggressive and chase the ball around. But when I saw my older brother getting money after every game, I realized I was missing out. I started getting more aggressive. I started caring about where that ball was going. And I started finding ways to get to the ball when it was near the goal. By the end of the year, I was averaging two or three goals a game. Within a few years, I was actually playing up two years on a team with my brother and outscoring everyone on the team. I'm sure that getting paid $1 a goal couldn't turn someone with zero abilities into the best soccer player on the team, but it did take someone who had the potential and force him to live up to it.

I'm not pretending for a second that giving away more prizes will turn everyone on your team into a rock star, but it will give motivation to the ones who are capable of becoming your next rock star. I hear people over and over saying that it's stupid to reward people for doing things they are supposed to do. My thoughts? Then why do jobs pay people and give them health benefits? Shouldn't we contribute to society because it's the right thing to do? We should, but I'm not planning on doing it without compensation.

I have mentored people in companies where the top leaders get rank advances. With some of the more important ranks, they get T-shirts, jackets, or even some type of elite status where they get to walk across a stage and get recognized in front of twenty thousand people. Those same leaders who worked their asses off for a jacket and a bouquet of flowers will claim that they shouldn't have to give out incentives to get others to do the work they are supposed to do. Interesting …

If motivation is understanding how people's thoughts and beliefs work, then try to remember that most people have been working their entire lives to try to earn the approval and recognition of others. If you understand this, why in the world wouldn't you use this to help people? If someone would show up more often with more smiles, more confidence, and more joy because you gave them a T-shirt, give them a damn T-shirt already!

Should people be willing to do it because it's the right thing to do? Sure. But why wouldn't you want them to feel that much more excited about doing the right thing? Why would you miss an opportunity to be the person who gets to create a lasting connection with them for being the first person since kindergarten who was willing to show them appreciation and give them the affirmation they have been secretly wanting for years?

MENTOR

Mentoring others can be one of the greatest gifts in life if you do it right, or the greatest curse if you do it wrong.

When you mentor the right people, you can pour your heart and soul into them, and it feels like they gave your time and energy right back to you. When you mentor the wrong people, it feels like every ounce of life and energy has been drained out of you. And that is why I teach about boundaries.

Motivation is a little more hands-off. I try to use my motivational gift for the masses. While I get my greatest ideas in one-on-one sessions, I try to limit those one-on-one sessions to one to three times a week. I have found that I can use my time more wisely when I put people into groups, where I'm teaching the same principles to many people at a time.

But mentorship is a different relationship altogether. Mentorship is when I choose someone that I honestly believe in enough that they have earned my time. Even in a business like mine, where I charge for this relationship, I don't take people into this space unless I know they're a good fit. If you are someone who plans to mentor others for free, you will need to learn my boundaries even more!

PERFORMANCE BASED

In 2016 I made a really important decision. I realized that I didn't enjoy life coaching for the sake of just growth; I wanted to take things a step further. In true life coaching, you show up for each call with your client and simply start the conversation with "What do you want to talk about today?" On one hand, I appreciated the art of true life coaching in that it was an organic process that allowed the person you're coaching to take the lead. This was the opposite of the mentorship I had grown up in, where you were supposed to copy the person that was mentoring you.

I realized that as long as the client had all of the control, they also had the ability to sabotage the process altogether. If there was something they knew they should have done that they didn't, they would just bring up something different to talk about. Some of my clients worked with me for months without really changing anything in their lives. Each session, they just brought up a new topic to avoid talking about the things they really needed to work on.

I decided that this was not good for me or my clients. They were paying me because it made them feel better about themselves to have a coach, but if they weren't actually progressing in life or business, they were really having a false sense of growth that kept them from facing the actual facts. The facts were that they were not growing, they were not changing, and they were not getting the end results that they said they wanted. This was also hurting me, because it was costing me precious time I could have been spending with people who could have been growing, making more money, and giving me positive testimonials.

When you work with the wrong people, you enable them and rob yourself. I actually want to take it a step further and say that you also rob your friends and loved ones. I want my business to make a difference in the world, but I've also made promises to my family to take care of them. Even if I'm getting paid to work with these clients, if they are draining my energy and holding me back from enjoying what I do, it means that I "clock out" from work each day with less energy and passion to give to my family.

Remember how I decided to change my business name to Josh Coats PUSH Coach and lost half my clients overnight? That hurt a little, but honestly it was needed. The people who didn't want to grow and reach big goals just didn't belong on my calendar. I started going on webinars and telling people that they shouldn't even sign up for my training unless they were ready to set big, scary goals and do the work it takes. I was surprised to see that my sales numbers actually went up. I learned such an incredible lesson about expectations.

I love to work out, which is probably why I get along so well with the health and fitness industry and mentor so many health coaches from different companies. I want you to imagine that one of my friends, let's say Robb, invites me over to watch a basketball game. I show up in my street clothes, wearing skinny jeans and a denim shirt. I walk in with a six-pack of local craft beer, pop one open, and hand it to him.

Robb says, "Hey, man, let's work out before we watch the game!"

Here I am on a Saturday night in my skinny jeans, one or two sips into my first beer. My answer is, "Hell no, man, I just want to chill tonight!"

Now let's change the situation a little. Let's pretend that Robb texts me on Friday and says, "Hey man, do you want to come over and watch the game tomorrow? I was thinking we could crush a workout together and then watch the game."

This time, I show up in my workout clothes, I bring some pre-workout with me, and I'm mentally prepared to work out like never before (my friend Robb is a beast) and then watch the game.

I'm not a lazy person just because in scenario one I didn't want to work out. That isn't what was communicated to me. I was just being a normal person who wanted to hang out.

Scenario two doesn't make me some type of extra-committed badass. The communication was just different.

I have seen a huge shift on social media over the past few years that really scares me. I see leaders posting 90 percent of the time about the trips, rewards, and perks of being an entrepreneur. Only 10 percent of the posts talk about the work it takes, the commitment needed, and the hustle you have to put in to earn those trips and rewards. Can you guess what my clients' biggest complaint is about the people who are joining their businesses?

"These people get excited for a month or two and then quit the minute it gets hard" is the complaint I hear over and over.

If you are building a *Bachelor* TV show business, meaning everything is an elaborate vacation, don't be surprised when the woman who gets the flower doesn't last when normal life hits.

Having a performance culture in your mentorship process is so important. It doesn't mean that everyone who joins will become your next rock star, but it definitely creates the right environment for someone to become your next rock star. That process starts with proper expectations. You would never put out an ad for the CEO of a company and only talk about the perks. You would also want them to know what the role is. You would want them to know what the culture is. You would want them to know what the expectations are and what you are hiring them to do.

Most people avoid this performance culture for two reasons. They are either people pleasers or people saviors, and sometimes both.

The people pleasers are so afraid of setting proper expectations because they are afraid that if they make the qualifications too hard, no one will show up. Here's the thing—if no one shows up, it just means you have more time to do the other things you need to do to take care of yourself, your health, and your business. Stop pretending that having the wrong people around is the same as making progress. When a sports team realizes they don't have the right pieces, they scratch the roster and start over. Continuing to pretend is only causing you more stress, and depleting you of your energy and confidence. The longer you try to save people, the longer you will find yourself failing as a leader and making yourself feel worse and worse about your own abilities to actually help people.

Repeat after me: It is better to be on the right mission by yourself than to be on the wrong mission with a group of people.

Imagine if you parented your kids from a people-pleasing mentality. Imagine that your kids never do their chores but still get their allowance because you don't want to make them mad. Would this be considered being a good parent? No. This is how we end up with spoiled brats who waste away generational wealth that someone else worked hard for. If you wouldn't raise your kids this way, please don't raise your team this way.

The second reason for avoiding a performance culture is what I call people-saving. People-saving has the appearance of performance, but it's quite the opposite. People-saving is when you care so much about people that you stop using any logic. You start trying to drag people along because of their perceived potential. Sometimes the potential you see is because of their personality type. Other times you see their potential because of something they achieved a long time ago, but the reality is they haven't done anything worthwhile in so long that you are just holding onto old memories.

Please remember, everyone in the world has the same level of potential. There isn't a person who has more potential. There are people with different gifts, and maybe some of those gifts are more suited for what you are needing right now. But talent does not equal success. Talent, combined with hard work and being coachable, is what determines someone's ability to succeed in any area of life.

On a scale of one to ten, ask yourself, *How hard do they work, and how coachable are they?* If the answer is nine or ten for both questions, then I would rather have that person than the person who is a ten in talent but doesn't work hard or listen to others.

I told one of my clients to write down on a piece of paper next to his computer: I am not Jesus, so it is not my job to save people.

I think it is a wonderful thing to want to help everyone. Maybe this simple idea will help you the same way it helped me in my first year of business. One of my mentors said, "If you spend your time helping the people who want your help, you can spend the rest of your life helping the people who need your help."

That was during a time that I was volunteering close to twenty hours a week at my local church. I was making a difference, and I really believed in the mission of the church. But this was a small church, and they couldn't afford to pay me for my time. I realized that as long as I was helping somewhere that couldn't pay me, I would have to work forty hours at a job I hated to afford the ability to volunteer somewhere I loved. What if instead of focusing so much on the people who needed me, I put my time into helping people who want my help and are willing to pay for it? If I could build a business helping people, I could work forty hours doing something I love and then volunteer any time I wanted because I would have so much energy and freedom.

Seven years later, I took that advice to the bank. I don't volunteer twenty hours a week, but my business is changing lives all over the world every day. When people locally want help or need advice, I'm happy to meet for coffee and volunteer my time. I no longer need money from anyone, so I get to help anytime and anywhere I want.

This performance mentality is one of the main ingredients in my PUSH Coach Certification School. It is a virtual school where you can learn the foundations of life coaching and learn everything I've added to it to make it more of a performance-based structure. As people are going through the training, they are seeing just how much more confidence they can have mentoring others when there is a plan in place to create structure, account-ability, and results. We have people going through the school to use this new way of coaching for business, health, and even corporate leadership. Life coaching really is the universal leadership tool. I have just taken that tool and made it more powerful and gave it more predictable results!

If you are someone interested in diving deeper into my leadership philosophies, make sure to grab my book *F*** Leadership*. If you want to become a master motivator and mentor, I highly recommend looking into my PUSH Coach Certification. You can get information on both of these resources at www.joshcoats.com.

COACHING QUESTIONS

1. Why do you think it's so important for leaders to be people who model the right behaviors?

2. In this chapter I talked about the three most important things to model: Actions, Energy, and Performance. List some things below that you need to step up in these areas.

Actions:

_____

Energy:

_____

Performance

_____

3. Fill in the blank: I have watched leader after leader try to "motivate" others by giving challenge after challenge, teaching after teaching, without addressing the most important issue:

_____

4. Why do you think we are so quick to try to fix behaviors without considering the beliefs that need to change first?

5. What are some of your best and worst memories of mentoring others?

6. What do the best memories have in common?

7. What do the worst memories have in common?

8. What can you learn from questions seven and eight about setting boundaries and expectations for future relationships?

Are you ready to step into becoming the best leader you could possibly imagine? The fastest way to do this is getting more hands-on coaching training. If you think you might be ready to start coaching others, go to https://www.joshcoats.com/survey to find out more about your leadership level and get some customized resources from my team!

9

SPIRITUALITY

I have to admit that as I'm typing this, I don't know which chapter this will be or exactly where it fits into this content; I just know it needs to be written. I grew up in the middle of the Bible Belt, and we always joked that if the middle of the country was the Bible Belt, Kansas and Oklahoma were like the buckle of the belt. A bigass brass buckle. LOL!

I grew up in a church that took that to an even further extreme. While it was basically the norm for most people I knew growing up to go to church every Sunday, we went to church Sunday morning, Sunday night, Wednesday night, and any weekend that there was a special event. We also had regular family prayer meetings where my dad would call the family together for situations that came up that were extra pressing that we needed to spend extra time praying over.

I don't mean saying grace over a meal. I mean spending a few hours lying on the ground, praying to God to open up the floodgates of heaven and pour out his blessings. Imagine being in the middle of watching your favorite show or being on the phone with your significant other, only to find out your dad wants to have an urgent prayer meeting.

Our church was very charismatic, and if you've ever watched the Tony Robbins special on Netflix, *I Am Not Your Guru* (2016) (which is amazing, btw), it was very similar to that. The only difference was, instead of people standing up to get coached, they would stand up to get prayed over, and it was considered a failure if the prayer wasn't powerful enough to knock the person down. And then, of course, at the end of the service, there was a big offering where we told people they needed to sow if they wanted to reap. It was very similar to the principle I taught in an earlier chapter, except that this was more of a guilt trip trying to get you to give all of your money to God so God would bless you back with a harvest. I had even heard of some preachers who were encouraging people to put money on a credit card if that's all they could do, to make sure God could give them a harvest.

Let me just say that, with as many crazy things I was taught, I was also taught enough good things to still have a very high level of respect for God and religion, and this chapter is in no way anti-religion. It is not meant to deter anyone from their religion or to encourage people to stop going to church, Mass, temple, or anything else that they consider sacred.

This chapter is not intended to take away your current perspective of religion or spirituality. The only goal of this book is to give you an additional perspective that might help you take a fresh look at spirituality through the eyes of your heart instead of the voices of your head. Remember, your heart is where you find pure love, purpose, and faith. Your head is where you find the voices of fear, shame, and guilt. If the heart speaks from abundance and the head speaks from scarcity, it seems like a great idea to make sure you see whatever version of an infinite spirit you believe in through your heart.

One of the reasons I fell in love with life coaching was because it gave me clarity for the very first time in my life about what God really wanted for my life. The church I grew up in had an obsession with hearing the voice of God and finding the will of God. While these are wonderful desires to have, I really want you to understand that you will never find God, the Universe, or whatever you believe in using your head. That can only be found in your heart.

Let's have another review of the head versus the heart. I want to share the graphic again so you can have a fresh look as we cover the same principle in a new area of life.

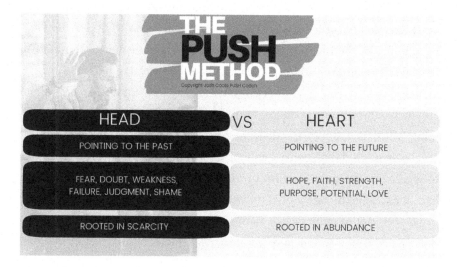

The head is always rooted in scarcity and pointing to the past. It expresses itself through fear, doubt, weakness, failure, judgment, and shame.

The heart is very different. It is rooted in abundance and always points to the future. It expresses itself through hope, faith, strength, purpose, potential, and love.

Life coaching taught me that I could find the voice or will of God at any time by simply looking at the right side of this chart and asking myself, *What would God's hope say about this?* or *What would God's faith say about this?* And I just go through each, one word at a time, until it really makes sense.

I stopped thinking so much about what was right and wrong and more about what was love and fear. I stopped thinking so much about whether people looked and sounded like me and started caring more about how they could become the best version of themselves. I started realizing that judgment and shame have no place in our hearts.

This doesn't mean that our heart has no regard for our health. While I don't believe our heart would ever shame us, I do believe that it challenges us, just in a different way. For instance, your heart might challenge you to start working out more if you realize that you want to improve your health.

But that is very different from shaming yourself for being overweight. Your heart may compel you to be more consistent with your business because it is challenging you to lean into strength, but that is very different from doubting yourself just because you have quit one hundred other times.

I once heard someone say that two-thirds of the word "God" is "Go." I think one of the biggest misunderstandings about God is to think it is a creature floating around in space, judging and criticizing people. I believe that God is an eternal spirit that possesses infinite love, infinite peace, infinite creativity, and infinite wisdom, and wants so much to simply share these things with you by allowing them to flow to you and through you.

I believe God is an eternal light of hope that is calling us to love, believe, forgive, and embrace. God isn't trying to hold you back from things you love, for God is the one who gave you that love.

God is not judging you or shaming you based on some rule or regulation that a human somewhere put into place. God cannot exist inside rules and has zero limits.

Every morning, as part of my routine, I start my journal and affirmation time by setting a timer for five minutes. I turn on some music and I say over and over, "I acknowledge my Creator today. I acknowledge the voice of my Creator today." And then I go through the words above. "I acknowledge the voice of hope in my life today. I acknowledge the voice of strength today. I acknowledge the voice of purpose today."

I start my day by becoming more aware of the abundance that lives on the inside of me. I then sit quietly, think through all of the good things I have in life, and simply say, "I am allowing more love in my life today. I am allowing more relationships today. I am allowing more health today. I am allowing more wealth today."

There is absolutely nothing wrong with the idea of religion, as long as you don't try to take heart issues and interpret them with your head. But I want you to be very aware of your own human nature, as well as the human nature of those who speak from stages. I want to just warn you that there are many people who come in the name of God and even have what they consider to be God-ordained credentials, but that doesn't mean they understand the difference between the heart and the head. Just because a man-made organization has approved them does not mean their words come from God.

I want to give you permission to explore spirituality from a new angle. I want to encourage you to let go of what you previously thought was "right and wrong" and instead pursue a life of love and purpose.

One of the biggest traps I fell into growing up was thinking that morals were the highest version of purpose. We would talk a lot about how God had a plan for everyone's life, but upon reflection, I realized that we spent so much time worrying about morals that they consumed our lives, leaving no room to pursue any type of purpose.

Living a moral life is not the overall purpose of your life. The overall purpose of your life is to reach your highest potential and to inspire others to do the same. Your purpose is to find the thing that makes you cry and makes you sing. Morals will easily fall into place when you know what you really want to do with your life. You'll never stay out all night drinking if you have something to wake up and do the next day. On the contrary, if you have nothing to do, I'm not sure what would keep you from staying out all night drinking. Preaching a moral code does not fix morals. Preaching purpose creates a need for personal morals.

Yesterday, I did what I call The Breakdown Session with my first round of students who are going through my Life Coach Certification program. I explained to them that I didn't want anyone going into the world endorsed by my name without being someone who has a larger-than-life purpose that they are willing to work for.

I walked them through the same series of questions I walk my one-on-one clients through on a first session. These questions are designed to help my clients dig in deep and find out what they really want in life. I'm so sick of people setting these smart goals that are supposed to be realistic and attainable. Have you ever studied a famous person who had a realistic goal? Was it realistic for Martin Luther King, Jr., through his leadership in the civil rights movement, to end legal segregation in the United States? He had everything going against him. But the size of his dream created the demand for his actions. And even though he didn't live to see the fuller fruition of his goals in this movement, he had a larger part than any other single human in bringing them about.

As I really dug in and kept asking over and over what they really wanted more than anything else in life, I finally saw what I wanted. They broke. I watched as, one at a time, the tears started to fall. One person wrote in the Zoom thread, "I want to build a six-figure business so I can bring my spouse home from his job that he hates." Another person wrote, "I want to start a nonprofit that changes lives all over the world." Another wrote, "I want to make enough money that I can show my children that they don't have to grow up suffering and can get what they want in life."

I then explained to them that they had just found their superpower. People don't change the world because they feel good or act good or have some superior level of morals and willpower. People change the world because they finally find something worth fighting for.

I spent thirty years of my life thinking that I had to somehow earn God's favor and try to keep Him/Her happy. Life coaching taught me that everything God has is already mine and He/She is just waiting for me to reach out and grab it. He/She is waiting for me to reach out and embrace it. But I can't do that as long as I'm spending all of my time trying to tell others why they aren't good enough to have it. I can't do that if I'm pointing fingers and trying to keep others out of the room.

You can't possibly create abundance in your own life while trying to hold others to something less.

Let me end this chapter by saying to anyone who has ever been judged or shamed by religion, I'm so sorry. Please know that, while I may have participated in that for the first thirty years of my life, I'm working very hard to change that. Please know that the voices of men and women against you are not the voices of God.

If you are reading this book, God has nothing but love, strength, hope, life, joy, purpose, and potential for your life. God is not limited by your gender, race, ethnicity, or sexual orientation. God is love. If you look at the world and see love, you have found God. Anywhere you see hatred, judgment, fear, or shame, I can promise that you are not looking at God.

This chapter is dedicated to my beautiful transgender child, Audrey. I'm so thankful that life coaching taught me these principles in time to prepare me to love *all* of my children exactly the way they are!

COACHING QUESTIONS

1. What is something you have been told about God and the Universe by other people who promote judgment and shame instead of love and acceptance?

   _____

   _____

   _____

2. What is something you have done that you thought was in the name of God and the Universe that you now realize was judgment and shame instead of love and acceptance?

   _____

   _____

   _____

3. What are some specific ways that you can show more love in your life to your family and friends? How can you show more love to strangers and enemies?

   _____

   _____

   _____

EPILOGUE

I'm not sure if you came to this book with a desire to help others or to improve your own life. My hope is that this material has inspired you to become the best version of yourself but also realize that there is an entire world that needs what you have to offer.

I will never forget the moment that I realized personal growth had completely wrecked my life (in a good way), and I just wanted to share it with everyone in the world. What started out as an intense desire to share what I was learning has grown into a worldwide movement.

I want to end this book by giving you a challenge. Please do not let the movement stop with you. If these chapters have challenged you, inspired you, or changed you for the better, ask yourself what you can do to pass it along. Maybe you get a copy of the book for everyone on your team, maybe you'll join my PUSH Coach Certification School to become a certified life coach, or maybe you just commit to having as many conversations as you can in coffee shops with people you already spend time with.

Whatever you do with this information, remember what I mentioned in an earlier chapter. Reprogramming happens with repetition and emotional experiences. I want to challenge you to read this book *three times* before you move on. That is how the content will get into your subconscious mind, where it actually becomes a part of you.

I don't want you to walk away just yet. The chapters you have read and the lessons you have learned are just now becoming real. What would happen if you took the lessons and systems I have spent seven years and thousands of clients developing and really embodied all of them in three months? Imagine if you could have the same growth over three months that took me seven years! What would that do to your life, your business, and your relationships?

Let me also say that the heart always comes from purpose and potential, never judgment and shame. So, if you don't have a desire to keep reading, please find a new book asap and just make sure to continue to learn. But if you know that this is a challenge that is awakening something in your purpose and potential, let's start over at chapter one and keep growing together!

One of my first assignments in my life coach program was to read a specific leadership book three times in a row and, to this day, I have taught and coached so many lessons from those twenty-one chapters. In fact, for my first few years, I could help any leader in any room by simply using coaching questions and pinpointing which leadership law they were struggling with.

What I love about the content of this book is that it is so universal to personal growth and achievement. These chapters will help you whether you are seeking to improve in your health, relationships, business, or anything else.

This book is a call to growth, from the inside out. I hope that you will take that call seriously. I hope that you will see, as I have over and over again, that all of life's problems can be solved by controlling the only thing you really can control: your own personal growth.

I know I might not know you, but I want to end this book the same way I end calls with my leadership groups.

I love you. I believe in you. You are worthy of everything you want in life. Please remember that everything you need is already living on the inside. And all of the resources you will ever need are right under your nose.

Your PUSH Coach,

Josh

Get your FREE signed copy
of the book, along with
the PDF workbook, at
www.joshcoats.com/newbook.

Get more details about my
Life Coach Certification at
www.joshcoats.com.